About the Author

Margaret spent many years bringing up her children and when they began to leave home she looked for another interest in her life. She investigated various job opportunities but soon realised that at the age of forty this was going to be difficult. Her previous knowledge was out-of-date and younger people were preferred. Slightly miffed to say the least she decided to employ herself! She has always enjoyed meeting new people and interacting with them and so she thought a B&B life might be a good venture in the meantime. When the 'Empty Nest' arrived, she decided to use the now spare bedrooms for Bed and Breakfast. This is the reason for many B&B startups. It was an experiment at first as she thought she would try it for six weeks to see what it was like to have strangers staying in her home. At the end of that time, she came to realise that she really enjoyed hearing about the lives of so many different people and who would ever have anticipated such entertainment?

Hard work it may be but the rewards were many and such enjoyment was really so unexpected.

To Maggie
Enjoy!
Margaret xx

There's Nowt So Strange as Folk

Margaret Martin

There's Nowt So Strange as Folk

Olympia Publishers
London

www.olympiapublishers.com
OLYMPIA PAPERBACK EDITION

Copyright © Margaret Martin 2023

The right of Margaret Martin to be identified as author of
this work has been asserted in accordance with sections 77 and 78
of the Copyright, Designs and Patents Act 1988.

All Rights Reserved

No reproduction, copy or transmission of this publication
may be made without written permission.
No paragraph of this publication may be reproduced,
copied or transmitted save with the written permission of the
publisher, or in accordance with the provisions
of the Copyright Act 1956 (as amended).

Any person who commits any unauthorised act in relation to
this publication may be liable to criminal
prosecution and civil claims for damage.

A CIP catalogue record for this title is
available from the British Library.

ISBN: 978-1-80074-335-9

This is a work of creative nonfiction. The events are portrayed to the
best of the author's memory. While all the stories in this book are
true, some names and identifying details have been changed to
protect the privacy of the people involved.

First Published in 2023

Olympia Publishers
Tallis House
2 Tallis Street
London
EC4Y 0AB

Printed in Great Britain

Dedication

I dedicate this book to all the wonderful people who have shared my home and enriched my life.

Acknowledgements

I've really enjoyed writing and remembering all these stories and I give thanks to my family and friends who encouraged me to put them all together.

Special thanks go to Marion Gibson – a long time 'B&Ber' who became my 'Guru' and started me off on this journey and to Barry Reilly of Computroon, who helped with laptop problems!

I can assure you that all of these wonderful stories all actually happened – good or bad!

Contents

INTRODUCTION 17
   In the Beginning 22
   First Guests 24

Chapter 1 26
   A Lovely Wedding Party 26
   A Young Interesting Wedding Guest 28
   Meet You in the Middle 30

Chapter 2 33
   Awkward Guy 33
   Smelly Simpson 35

Chapter 3 37
   C'mon Aatha! 37

Chapter 4 43
   The First and Hopefully the Last! 43

Chapter 5 46
   Filipinos 46

Chapter 6 51
Strange People 51
Wuxing – no, not waxing – wuxing! 52
The Miseries 54
Poltergeist 58

Chapter 7 60
Reiki 60
Yoga 62
Hypnosis 62
This Is Someone Who Really Needed To Relax! 64

Chapter 8 67
Chess Chumps 67
Strange Names 69
You Cannot Be Serious 71

Chapter 9 73
For This One Make Up Your Own Mind! 73
Odd Balls 75
Harry the Walker – Another O. B. 77
Another Walker 79

Chapter 10 83
The Flower Club 83
Lawnmower 84
The Wedding Anniversary 86

Chapter 11 91
  Arrival Times 91
  An Unhappy Lady 95

Chapter 12 97
  Employing the Family 97
  The Tourist Board Inspection 98
  Last Inspection 102
  Panic Abroad 104

Chapter 13 108
  Another Key Story 108
  More Keys 111

Chapter 14 115
  Americans 115
  More Golfers 117

Chapter 15 120
  Bonuses 120

Chapter 16 124
  There's Always Some! 124

Chapter 17 130
  Damages 130
  More 131

Toilet Seat..132
　　Hidden Damage 134

Chapter 18 138
　　Open Offences..138

Chapter 19 143
　　The French Girls From Hell! 143

Chapter 20 152
　　Dogs..152
　　Young Ones 154

Chapter 21 158
　　The Nasties!..158

Chapter 22 163
　　A Referral 163
　　Mother and Dancer Daughter 164

Chapter 23 169
　　A Tail to Tell!..169
　　Naughty Otto!..173

Chapter 24 176
　　Jammies 176
　　Me Again!..177
　　Why Did the Woman NOT Cross the Road? 178
　　Another Very Strong Character.................................184

Chapter 25 187
　　My Availability 187

Internet Dating 188
Date Night 190
The Monkees 192

Chapter 26 194
Woman From the 'Evil' Town 194

Chapter 27 198
Wow – Be Grateful for Your Life 198

Chapter 28 201
Almost a Lodger 201

Chapter 29 209
Diets and Nice People 209

Chapter 30 218
Sock Droppings 218
Bikers – Fluff? 218

Chapter 31 224
Familiarisation Visits 224
Culzean Castle 226
Ailsa Craig 227
The Isle of Arran 227

Chapter 32 231
Princess Scota 231

Chapter 33 238
    Four in a Bed 238

Chapter 34 241
    NASA 241

Chapter 35 243
    Bed and Breakfast Worldwide 243

INTRODUCTION

There's Nowt So Strange as Folk! – how true this is! From my years of running a B&B from my home I am now not surprised at anything anyone will do or tell me! I am convinced that everyone is slightly mad (except me!). Almost everyone has a story to tell and is more than willing to tell it.

I would not have believed that such an ordinary and supposedly mundane 'job' would yield such extraordinary and entertaining experiences.

This surprised me as I'm not sure I would be as willing to reveal to strangers, details of my life like some people are so keen to do. Also, it's not just single people who, being on their own, feel the need to share their lives but couples and families alike. I did not expect this, but I must say I found it really interesting. They are also interested in me and my family although I do not go into nearly as much detail!

I had not 'worked' for twenty years whilst bringing up my children. I was a typical housewife of my generation and looked after my family while my husband went out to work. He went to work, and I did everything else! I accepted this as my mother before me, as did most mothers, but I did feel like I was a 'kept woman' who did not contribute to the family's finances. Like my mother I had no money of my own as my job had been low paid in those days and of course when you became pregnant most women stopped work completely.

When my older children reached an age of semi-independence, both having left home for university, I felt the need to have something else in my life. I tried for several jobs with great enthusiasm but found to my disgust that already at the age of forty I was deemed too old to be of much use. Not only that, as I wanted to work part time in order to still collect my youngest from school etc., I found that the pay was such that I would be using it all up to pay for a child minder and so there was not much point. There were not many nurseries then and they would be expensive too.

I did, however, go for several interviews and got on well with the interviewers but each time I had the impression that they were just going through the motions. Sure enough, each job was given to a younger person. Could they not think along the lines of which one of us (if female) was going to get married and possibly leave soon? Which one of us had more life experience and job experience? Such short sightedness! Don't these people (mostly younger than me!) know that life experience makes a person more reliable, works harder, is willing and interested in the job and less likely to bunk off on pre-texts? Well, OK then, if they can't see my worth, I will employ myself! The family was encouraging, and my husband was OK with it as long as it didn't involve him! Extra money would be very welcome and cover family holiday costs. At long last I could contribute! Great idea!

Utilise my assets, that's what I will do! The house has three empty bedrooms therefore I can become a 'Seaside Landlady!'

Being in a residential part of town is not the optimum location for a B&B. If you are in a rural or urban town then a centre location is best. In a seaside town then the sea or beach front wins hands down. Everyone likes a great view. In any event the best sites are on a main road where the most number of people will be passing your door. A prominent sign in the garden is then the magnet for visitors. As we were not on a main road for passing trade, I had to rely on the tourist board initially then referrals from B&Bs which were full in the town then of course the internet made bookings a lot easier. Although we had few people knocking on our door (unless they had been told of us by people in the town) I actually liked the fact that I did not have to decide on the doorstep whether to let people in or not. With phone bookings or via the internet you can find out more about the people before they arrive.

With great enthusiasm I took many photographs of my rooms, the house and the gardens. I learned that if you put on all the lights in the rooms then the pictures are much better when lit. I sent them over to the tourist board for publication on their websites and had a website created on the internet. I found that there are many area and regional websites where you can advertise for free so I signed up with as many as I could find, and also found a selection who charged a small annual fee. When people called to book, I would ask them where they found us and that way could find out which websites were working for us. Unexpectedly, some paid websites were not necessarily the best for numbers of bookings.

I had some business cards printed and gave them out to guests when they paid their bill. Quite soon I decided that a brochure would be a good way to spread the word too as they could keep it for next time and give it to friends if they were coming this way. While looking for a company to print these the 'angels' stepped in! I had a guest who booked in from Inverness. He was here for a few days looking for clients and delivering orders that he had fulfilled for this area. It turned out that he was a publisher of tourist leaflets and brochures! I asked him for details of what he could do, and he created a triple folded brochure of my B&B, and it also incorporated my self-catering apartment. I was delighted with it and years later had him do an updated one.

In the beginning my downstairs room had no ensuite – it was not the norm in those days. The guests had to come out of the bedroom and cross the hallway to the little cloakroom off the hall. After a few months I installed a wash hand basin in that bedroom. This was then described as 'having hot and cold' but they still had to go across to the toilet! Unthinkable nowadays!

It was not long before I had an ensuite bathroom (full bathroom plus shower) added on to the room as there was enough space with the room being on the ground floor and having an outside wall to it. Now I felt it was a professional business!

With the local tourist office opening less and less hours the visitor numbers were falling. When the opening hours came down to only ten a.m. to two p.m. I decided to do something about it. It seemed that closure of the office was looming with the excuse being that 'there were not enough visitors to support the office'. Given that it was only open during lunch time then no wonder the numbers were down. I organised a petition questionnaire and each B&B gave their guests one to fill out. It had ten questions to answer e.g., asking did they think a TIC (Tourist Information Centre) was necessary, had they visited it, what hours should it be open, how many days a week etc. A hundred questionnaires were sent to the tourist board, all saying how useful an office it was but of course, these were ignored and it closed anyway. Now the nearest office is Glasgow (or the Isle of Arran). Plus ca change!

I started off in a small way to see if I liked it and how it would work out.

My mother was not keen at all on the idea as she had the old image that a B&B was a 'boarding house' and a very down-market business with bare rooms, very basic facilities and very dodgy clients. Anyone booking in would be down on their luck and I would have to keep an eye on everything portable! I tried to tell her that it had not been like that for many years and now B&B was seen by many as a way of avoiding hotel 'sameness' and being very impersonal. People from overseas appreciate seeing the way of life to be experienced in a different country. They enjoy the fact that the locals give them so much information of the surrounding area and have helpful suggestions about where to visit and where to eat. If language is a problem, it's amazing how much you can convey with sign language and that can be fun and funny too. Happily, my son married a lovely French girl, and with her parents having no English and my schoolgirl French to get by on that was all useful many times. People from Denmark, Sweden, China and even Iceland posed more of a problem! There again sign language helps! However, most people have at least one person in their party who can speak enough English and be their spokesperson.

Mother was not convinced but over the years she became

more accepting and having met some of the guests she realised they were quite normal and nice people and when I slipped in the fact sometimes that 'Dr' so and so and Professor this was coming she mollified quite a bit. When a top lawyer and a well-known singer came to stay then she had to accept that B&B was different nowadays.

To start a B&B minimum expenditure is required, and so this seemed like a good business to try. I could get a few new towels, bed linen, table linen, which I could do with anyway, and hospitality trays. Easy stuff. I was soon to learn that that indeed was the easy bit!

In the Beginning

It was a year when the British Open Golf Championship was being held in town. Many people who do not usually do B&B were renting out rooms for the duration of the championship. Even driveways were rented out as there is limited parking at the course. Although I had missed it for that year it gave me the idea. I would try it for six weeks to see if I liked it. The rest, as they say, is history!

To find out what I had to do I telephoned the local tourist board. In those days we had a local tourist board, whereas now these have been done away with as the powers that be have decided that these offices are unnecessary and expensive because most people find accommodation and information on the internet. All accommodation providers are enraged at this because a tourist office shouldn't be seen as an expense but the service that it is. Yes, people may book via the internet but after arriving at their chosen destination they will go to the tourist office to gain more information and local knowledge. I have questioned those at the top as to where the first place is that they go to when they visit a new place in a new country? Needless to say, their 'strategy' does not recognise this.

The reality is that if there is no tourist office nearby then people will think that there cannot be anything to see or do there so they will go somewhere else! Just take The Isle of Sky, Arran, and cities like Edinburgh and Glasgow as an example. The offices there are extremely busy.

So, despite this, I told the then tourist board that I was thinking about doing B&B and wondered how to get started.

"Just pay the membership and we will advertise your property in our brochures," was the reply to my query.

"When will you come and inspect my property?"

"Oh, we don't inspect unless a complaint is received," was the unexpected reply! They were quite happy to advertise my property without knowing anything about it! I was astounded. I might have had a filthy place and be infested with fleas! Nowadays it's different with the quality and grading system for members but back in the 80s this was not enforced. As many places did not have high standards, the tourist boards soon realised, they were having too many complaints coming back to them as they were the organisation who had booked in the guests. This led to the introduction of the grading system of star awards for tourist board members. A visit from the inspector, always incognito, led to the award of one to five stars for each property. Thereafter an annual inspection was done and not always incognito. Expecting an inspection is always stressful as every booking for a single person (usually a woman) results in wondering if it is the inspector and trying not to have a 'Faulty Towers' experience for them! It's amazing how when you need to have a good regime going you seem to have unexpected problems like the toaster not working or spilling the juice or milk or burning the breakfast!

So, I paid my fee...

The first few guest experiences were uneventful, and I settled into a routine of happy letting. As time went on more and more people became interesting and some extremely noteworthy to the point when I thought, I should write these down – truth is stranger than fiction. So, I did!

<u>First Guests</u>

Having cleaned my place and weeded the garden to an inch of its life I awaited my first guests with a large amount of trepidation. My ideal first timers, I thought, would be a nice couple of tourists to practise on...

In reality, the tourist board telephoned me to ask if I could take five people and a dog!

Cough. "Yes, fine... When will they arrive?"

"They'll be right up!" Gulp.

About ten minutes later a car drove into the driveway. I could feel my heart rate rising dramatically I was so nervous! Just keep thinking, I told myself, five x £12! – a goodly amount in those days, at least to me, as I hadn't earned any money of my own for so long! I watched from the kitchen window as they brought out their luggage (plus dog) and approached the front door. They were very nice and appreciative of the place and the dog was quite docile and friendly (until it saw the cat, but that is another story!).

Although I offer a range of options for breakfast, they all actually wanted the same thing – "The Full Scottish". Later on, I would say to people when they asked for "The Full

English", I would say with a sad face, "Sorry I don't do a Full English," and then when they didn't know what to say I would smile and say, "but I can do 'The Full Scottish!'" then explain the difference. The Full English is bacon, egg, sausage, tomato, mushrooms and baked beans. The Full Scottish is the same but substituting the beans for a potato scone (then having to explain what a potato (tattie) scone is!). This being a flat potato cake fried and particularly delicious with tomato and bacon.

For my first breakfast all went smoothly. Everything was fine with no burnt offerings. They were chatting happily and commenting on how nice everything was and what a pleasant place to stay. I must say I appreciated that after all my efforts though I didn't tell them they were my first visitors ever! On leaving they handed me payment in cash with their thanks and hoped they would be back again some time. I smiled and said I hoped so and waved them off. I waited until they had left the driveway then closed the door and let out a whoop and threw the notes (all £60!) up in the air and let them flutter down around me grinning like a mad thing (yes, maybe I'm mad too!). Euphoric! I was hooked! Is this all there is to it? Let nice people sleep in my spare rooms and get paid for it? Oh, yes, bring it on!

Well, yes, and no…

Chapter 1

<u>A Lovely Wedding Party</u>

Wedding guests are common in B&Bs, but the family involved usually stay in the hotel where the reception is being held or in the homes of the bride or groom. The mother of this lovely bride and groom visited several guest houses in this area to find a place suitable for the bride to leave from which also had gardens for the photographs. Happily, The Cherries was chosen for its private gardens, and having only four letting rooms they could take over the house almost as their own as we would keep in the background but help out if and when needed.

    Five days before the event a basket of flowers was delivered for the bride in the morning, and she arrived in the afternoon with her sister, maid of honour, and mother and father. Mother was obviously very excited and talked nonstop. Father was very laid back, being supportive but taking a non-active part in arrangements in usual father style. He took the opportunity to indulge in several rounds of golf during the pre-wedding days. The groom joined him a couple of times and they were all obviously a close and loving family.

    The weather was perfect the whole time making it even more special as prior to those days we had had the wettest summer on record!

The day before the wedding the family and a few friends had a champagne sandwich lunch in our back garden, and I supplied the tea and took some photos for them.

The morning of the big day was celebrated with more champagne at breakfast to which I was invited. The ironing board was in full use and when everyone was dressed, they all assembled for photos in the gardens. The official photographer arrived and while she was busy, I photographed them being photographed!

Even the cat got in on the act and the tiny bridesmaids who had arrived for the photos kept escaping to play with her and that too got photographed!

The cars arrived and made a splendid sight in the driveway. The bride's car was a vintage Rolls Royce matching the colour of her bouquet and the car for the mother and the bridesmaids was the large modern version decorated with white ribbons. All cameras were working overtime!

The parents returned the next night and said how well everything had worked out and how happy they were.

We too enjoyed their special day and were happy they chose The Cherries!

Another wonderful wedding was when a French couple came here to get married. They were a very good-looking couple both having a second marriage and had chosen Scotland because they had been over a few years previously and had fallen in love with the country and vowed that when they married it would be here. They only had a little English and although I have a little French, I had to get help in communicating with them from my English–French dictionary, my computer, and my son and daughter in law who were then living in France. With one day's notice the groom asked me if I could find a burgundy limousine (to match the burgundy accessories of the bride's dress) to collect the two of them on the day. Wow, at such short notice that was a tall order! Amazingly, after many phone calls, I found one. The big day dawned bright and sunny, and the bride was truly stunning. Her dress was pale cream and slim and extremely elegant with a small train. It had a corset laced top and the back lacing was in the burgundy colour. She wore a straw hat with burgundy ribbons. The look was completed by long cream gloves. I have a beautiful photograph of her standing at my front door looking backwards. Wonderful! She had two sons from her previous marriage aged fourteen and the groom had a son of about twelve. They all wore cream suits.

I was invited to the wedding which was held in an old church surrounded by an ancient graveyard and ruins and it was very atmospheric. The wedding itself was very informal and in fact the groom was seen upstairs in the gallery taking pictures! Just a handful of people were present and so it was all very friendly. The ceremony was conducted in French and English.

When they all returned to France, they sent me pictures and said they would return for their first anniversary which they did.

A Young Interesting Wedding Guest

A single girl around twenty-five years of age came here for one night for a wedding reception at a nearby hotel. She wasn't sure what time she would arrive as the wedding was in Glasgow and the reception was here by the sea. She said she was still sailing so was not sure when she would get here. She was still sailing? Was she on a yacht? A small one, or a large one? It was early April, and we were having one of the coldest Aprils on record. Maybe she was just coming on the Irish ferry?

The next day she called in the afternoon and arrived to check in with her bag – just ten minutes before the wedding breakfast was due to start at the hotel. This is typical of young ones and a good job I was in! She changed quickly and I gave her a lift to the venue.

She was a very nice bright young woman with a zest for life. Her 'sailing' she told me was that she worked on a supply ship in the North Sea and was training to join the merchant navy. So, she didn't sail into the harbour here at all as she had taken a train from the east coast.

"Oh," I said. "Lots of nice guys to work with then?"

"Oh yes," she said, "it's great!"

"How many women are there on board?"

"Just me!"

"Wow, and how many men?"

"Fourteen."

"And do they treat you any differently because you are a woman? How do you get on with them?"

"No, they are very good, and we get on really well. No bitching like women can often do. I was surprised at the beginning at the fact that the guys didn't offer to help if I was doing heavy lifting or a difficult manoeuvre."

I asked her how she got into this job, and she said that although she came from Glasgow, she had got a summer job on board a fishing boat based up north at Mallaig just across from the Isle of Skye. She also went diving for clams for extra money. She had come to the conclusion that divers are all slightly mad perhaps due to constant pressure on the brain and abnormal breathing conditions. This had really concerned her and so she had joined the cadet ship for training and had her sights set on being a captain one day. In the meantime, she was on board for six weeks at a time and sailing in and out of Aberdeen to the oil rigs to take them supplies.

She was very brave taking a job in such a man's world and was really enjoying the challenge.

Good luck to her I say!

Meet You in the Middle

A couple moved into a house half-way down our street. Not long afterwards I was going round the doors collecting for charity when I noticed in their glass entrance porch that there was a board lying against a chair and there was a name plate for B&B and the name of their house was on it. As they weren't in, I thought I must come back and introduce myself and see if they would like to join our local tourist association as I was on the committee. I would tell them that this organisation was very useful for listing vacancies, keeping up with local news and events and learning the name of anyone who has damaged a property or left without paying.

Some days later I called in to meet these new people. They laughed when I said why I was there as they didn't do B&B at all but friends had given them the board as a joke because they knew that the couple were constantly having friends over and so they thought it was an appropriate hostess gift thinking they would appreciate it, which they did. We all clicked instantly and became close friends. They actually decided to do B&B after this – after all, they had the sign! They joined the association too and far from being competition for me we found it was very useful as most B&Bs do not have many rooms especially if it is a family home and so if a party consists of six or more then we share the booking and the guests are happy because they can just walk down the road to meet up with each other. This is great for parties who are coming for a wedding or a birthday party, anniversary or a funeral, for example.

Sometimes if guests arrive unexpectedly and either of us is short of an egg, sausage or whatever in the morning then rather than rushing out to the local shop we can phone each other and say 'Can you give me any bacon, egg?' etc. This resulted in our beloved 'Meet you in the middle!' We would come out and trot quickly down the middle of the road (not on the pavement!) towards each other with arms outstretched carrying the required item and when we met, we hugged, handed over the item, turned and quickly trotted back shouting see you soon, and waving. We loved that! Actually, when they moved away south to be nearer their family, they came back up one time to visit and brought with them a sausage with a yellow ribbon wrapped around it!

Another benefit of having them down the road was if either of us needed help. A memorable help for me was when I accepted a booking of six men coming for a golf weekend. What was I thinking?

They arrived all very jolly and so excited at being 'away from the missus' for a whole weekend. Alarm bells began to ring in my head. They went off by taxi to eat then were going to the pub afterwards. At about nine p.m. one of them arrived here having walked back from the town. He was ten sheets to the wind and staggered in slurring, "Hello, Daahling!" then shuffled into his room which was luckily not upstairs. I was worried that he would damage the room (by several means!).

From my bedroom, which is upstairs, I can actually see down to the window of that room, so I went up there to see how he was. I saw him go and sit on the single bed then slide off it on to the floor. Oh dear, I thought, this is only nine p.m. what will the others be like if they don't come back till midnight or even later?

I called Harry down the road (my husband was away as he travelled a lot) and told him the situation. I asked if he would come and sit with me till they came back. Bless his heart he did, and they came back about eleven p.m. and were actually fine as they were here to play golf not to get 'bladdered' Phew!

In the morning the drunken one apologised and explained that he had problems at home and the freedom had just gone to his head. Thankfully there was no damage done to the room. He also bought a gift for his wife from the souvenir table which I had set up in my lounge with tourist information and Scottish gifts. I hope they resolved whatever problem they had!

Chapter 2

Awkward Guy

You call people strange if they are different to you but sometimes it is just a culture thing.

This man was put on to me by a local agency as there was a horse racing weekend on in the next town of Ayr. Most B&Bs were full and as he was starting work at the hospital in Ayr he needed accommodation. As I had a room till the end of the week, I accepted him.

What the agency didn't tell me was that he didn't have a car. This is not always a problem for visitors because restaurants are only a fifteen-minute walk away but for him working, it was not easy to get to the hospital from here. We are half a mile from the main road and the buses there are not a frequent service.

The first thing was that he arrived when I was out. I had been told that he would arrive at five p.m. and when I came home around three p.m. there he was on the doorstep! What a good job I was not staying out till much later! He was obviously put out at this, and when I showed him to his single room he said he was expecting a double bed. I told him that the only room with a double bed was the large family room but that would be more expensive for single use. He did not want to pay the extra. He was also not happy with the fact that he would have to share two bathrooms with one twin room if anyone booked in. The agency had not told him that.

He was a doctor from India and as he would be working long and irregular hours he needed to be near the hospital. The agency really messed things up but perhaps were struggling as the area was very busy because of the racing. I found out later that the hospital had given him a room in staff quarters, but it was a single bed too, shared bathrooms and shared kitchen facilities. He had walked out of there to find better accommodation.

He wanted me to run him across to the hospital and seemed surprised when I said that I could not do that as I had to be here for other guests arriving.

What did his last slave die of?

I suggested either the train (I could run him quickly to the station) or a taxi. He complained at the price of the taxi which he had taken to get here, believing that he had been ripped off, but, no I told him that that was the normal price. He asked me to phone around for alternative accommodation (again) which I did but, in the end, I had to give up. I trekked back upstairs to tell him this only to find that he had been on to Google and found a self-catering apt near the hospital! Thanks for telling me you were doing that! He stayed one night then moved out. He obviously did have plenty of money as the apartment he had found was not cheap and also, he had told me that he regularly sends sacks of sugar home to be distributed to the poor at home. Why sugar and not flour I asked him? He said that they were not short of flour and with sugar they could put it into orange juice for energy and vitamins. As a doctor I was surprised that he would use sugar like that. Healthy?

In subsequent conversation I asked what his speciality was, and he told me that it was general medicine.

I just hoped that I was never referred to him for any reason!

I wonder if he is still complaining – hospital food, long hours, lazy nurses, old equipment…

Smelly Simpson
Sometimes you give people nicknames which you keep to yourself, with no disrespect to those people, it just helps to identify them on repeat visits. Smelly Simpson was one of them. He came by himself several times over the years. He liked to come by train as he was a self-professed train spotter. Although I always asked him for the time of his arrival so that I could collect him from the station, most of the time he took a different train as he got distracted by all the trains that he had not catalogued. Many times I would find him on my doorstep. (He was not bothered – see later!) He came up from Oxford and always carried the same bag. It was a plastic white and green holdall with writing advertising soup. I think I had won the same thing in a competition some years ago!

He usually stayed three or four days and spent his time on the local trains. He was not one for long conversations and so I left him to enjoy his stay. The first morning I went into his room to do room service after he had gone out (carrying his soup holdall) and I was aware of a quite unidentifiable smell. It was not pleasant or particularly unpleasant. It was not any toiletry or smoke or anything bad, just strange and it filled the room although luckily it did not permeate through the house. No, it was not pot either! He was always very clean and tidy so I couldn't fathom out what it was, nor did I feel like asking him! The bedding had a slight smell of it but that would be being changed anyway. When he left and I had cleaned the room the smell went away quite quickly.

The last year he came he brought his wife with him. She did not seem happy with the place, and she did not chat either. A few days after they had left, she sent me a letter complaining about several things. She never mentioned anything while they were here. She said the room kettle was dangerous (it wasn't), the hospitality tray was not high enough for her, no Rooibos tea, (could have asked for some!) and the place was too far from the station. Well, it wasn't for her husband, or he would not have kept coming back! If people are not happy then they should tell their host and nine times out of ten the problem will be sorted.

Poor Smelly Simpson, he never returned! He was probably too embarrassed!

By the way, I have since discovered that some medications can make some people smell quite strongly! My husband had a spell of having a medication that made him smell a bit like that.

The things you learn!

Chapter 3

C'mon Aatha!

This tale happened not long after the arrival of the first five people and their dog. These new people were absolutely unique and such a joy that they set the standard for entertainment to an incomparable level.

They also were booked in by the local tourist board. Having taken the booking for four nights I went to check that the room was ready for them. The phone rang and it was the woman from the tourist office again who said she had been asked by the guests to apologise for the state of the man as he and his wife (plus dog) had spent the night in the car and so he had not had the chance to shave. No problem (why would it be?).

Half an hour later they still had not arrived. I phoned the tourist office to see if they had changed their plans.

"No," she said, "as far as I know they were coming straight over to you."

Another fifteen minutes went by and then I heard a car coming very slowly along the road as if looking for the house. This must be them. Sure enough, the car slowly drove into the driveway and I saw just why they had taken so long to arrive. The car was a very, very old Cortina and the suspension was nearly on the ground! They were also pulling a three-wheel canvas covered trailer, but the interesting thing was on the roof of the car. There was an aluminium bucket attached to the roof rack. Not, as you would expect, upside down for stability but upright. I later discovered it was full of water to top up the car radiator! That was why they were going so slowly. You couldn't make it up!

The couple (plus dog) came in and were quite a spectacle. Yes, the guy was unshaven, but it seemed to go with his wild hair, checked shirt and trouser belt which was so long the end of it hung down to his knees! All this and the fact that he was over six foot tall and even facially he was a dead ringer for Patrick Moore, the famous, popular, unkempt TV astronomer. The woman's outfit was straight out of the 60s, luminous pink and orange socks and plastic popper beads and beehive hairdo! Fabulous!

They introduced themselves as Ruby and Arthur from Lancashire and had that wonderful accent. Ruby did ninety-nine per cent of the talking and seemed entranced by our B&B. Everything was "Loovely" or "Gawjus." This was always followed by, "In'it, AAtha?" I led them upstairs with Ruby again, "Oooh, this is gawjus, in'it, Aaatha?" and then as she followed me, she encouraged Arthur to, "C'mon, Aatha!"

I left them to settle in having agreed to charge for the dog. I never charge for dogs at all, but Ruby insisted on £5 per night as, "He is our baby, and we want to pay for him." OK…

At breakfast, with no one else at the table, Ruby asked me if I would like to see photos of their aviary. Little did I know that this would turn out to be the most hysterical conversation I've ever had!

"We've had this aviary for some years now, 'aven't we, Aatha?" Arthur nods.

"My boss knew about it and asked me one day if I would like some chickens? 'Ooooh, yes ah said, and we could get some eggs from 'em too.' So, I got these four chickens and as they grew, we realised there were three 'ens and a cock. Ooooh, Aatha! The cock was beeyutiful, wasn' e, Aatha?" Arthur nods.

"Yes, his neck feathers became black, green and shiny purple, jus gawjus, din' they, Aatha?" more nods.

"Right, well, we noticed that the cock – we called him Joseph you know, because of his multi-coloured coat – was very friendly with one of the 'ens. Then, later on, we found she had laid an egg. Oooh, Maaagret!

It was near to hatching and when I told my boss at work he said, "Well, Ruby, you have to name your new chick and with your name, there is only one choice."

"What's that then?" I asked 'im.

"You are Ruby, so the chick must be Emerald!"

"That were perrrrfect, so we did. Mother 'en were named Amber."

Ruby showed me pictures of Joseph and yes, he did look very colourful and grand. Amber and Emerald were 'so cute'.

Then Ruby started telling me where she worked. It was at the Beecham's factory near Blackpool, and she cycled there every day over small country roads, her basket fixed in front. One day she was cycling along when a large lorry came up behind her and the driver leaned on his horn.

"Well, Ah nearly fell off me bike din ah, Maagret? Booger 'im a thought ah've as much right as 'im to road so ah'm not letting 'im by! This went on for a few miles to main road with 'im giving me the horn and me giving 'im the finger!"

She took breath and then said, "Aatha, go get Maagret some Bovril cubes – do you like Bovril, Maagret?"

"Err, yes," I said.

"They make Bovril cubes now you know, just like Oxo cubes you know. Go on Aatha, you'll find 'em in the front pocket of the car."

Arthur duly moseyed off to the car and came back with a dog-eared packet which looked like it had been in the car for years.

"Thank you so much," I said politely.

Ruby was a sight to behold that morning. Her usual purple popper beads round her neck, the beehive hairdo, a luminous lime green T-shirt and luminous pink socks with plimsolls with an orange flash on them. Brilliant!

After breakfast they were going off to Edinburgh (leaving the trailer). Ruby had always wanted a tartan skirt, "Din' ah, Aatha?" and so Arthur had promised her one from Edinburgh. Off they went at the usual twenty miles per hour. I wondered whether they would be back that night!

Sure enough, they made it back at night complete with the tartan skirt. Arthur didn't 'do shopping' so he waited for Ruby in the Princes Street gardens. When they got back it was so late there was only one place open to eat – the most expensive place in town!

Ruby had said, "Ooh, Aatha, Ah can't go in ther, ah'm wearing me rainmate and plastic mac!" (It was pouring with rain.)

"Have to," said Arthur and so removing the rainmate they went in and were shown to a table in the middle of the room. This made Ruby feel even more conspicuous and when the very large menu folder arrived, she hid behind it. Peeking round it, she whispered to Arthur, "See the prices?"

"Just have an omelette," said Arthur.

Suddenly, while they were eating, there was the sound of cars colliding outside and amazingly Arthur leapt up, ran out and when he saw the two cars locked together and steaming, he shouted, "Get out, get out." He also shouted to the drivers to open the hoods and then he managed somehow to remove the batteries to prevent fire.

"I learnt that in the army," he said. Good old Arthur!

On leaving they paid up and also for the dog 'nine bells' (apparently had knocked nine bells out of his ball when he was a puppy!) and the parting statement from Ruby was, "Ah were going to leave you a plastic dog turd on the carpet in our room, Maagret, but Aatha said that weren't a good idea. I thought you would have appreciated the joke, Maagret."

Good old Arthur once again!
I really missed their stories and Ooh Aathas!

The Electric Brae

There is a very interesting geographical phenomenon in Ayrshire called the Electric Brae. It is on the coastal road from Ayr to Culzean Castle and is a natural tourist attraction. It has confounded visitors and locals alike for hundreds of years. It is a section of the road which appears to be on a hill but very strangely the hill is back to front as cars, buses, balls, bottles etc, all roll 'uphill'. At any time of the year, you will see cars stopped at this stretch to test this out. People watch as their cars roll uphill and children love putting their tennis/golf/rubber balls on the road to see them go uphill.

I had a family staying for a holiday weekend and they had found out about the Electric Brae on the internet. They asked directions to it and the father of the family was determined to suss out what this was all about. I'm sure he didn't believe it was for real.

The next morning at the table they were full of the story and had even filmed their car going 'uphill'. They had stopped the car, taken the hand brake off and couldn't believe it when the car started rolling. Mother kept saying, "It was amazing!"

Father had looked underneath the car to see whether the road was flat, "No, it was definitely sloping!" He then put an empty juice bottle on the road, and it took off rolling over and over 'uphill'.

They stopped the car at different parts of the road and each time it rolled up hill again.

There is a stone monument to this Brae in the lay-by to tell people where to start the roll and the theories behind it.

I can just imagine the copious, "Ooh Aathas," that would have come from Ruby if they had seen that!

Chapter 4

<u>The First and Hopefully the Last!</u>

Sometimes a story lands on your doorstep and you think, "You couldn't imagine this happening."

A mother from Northern Ireland phoned to book in two 'lads' for one night, arrival time eight thirty p.m.

As the Irish ferry was due in around seven thirty p.m. and is only a five-minute drive from here there was plenty of time for them to arrive even if there had been adverse weather conditions to delay the boat. Not applicable in this case. Nine thirty p.m. came and went and at ten fifteen p.m. as I did not have their mobile phone number, I phoned the mother to check if they were still coming.

"Yes," she said, "they have likely gone to have something to eat."

They might have checked in first so I could have gone to bed!

She then informed me (as if it was relevant to them being late), that they were funeral directors and were collecting remains to be taken back to Northern Ireland. I was tired, I didn't ask...

She said she would call them. She, not them, called me back and said they were at some hospital (I didn't catch the name so I had no idea where they were) and would be here in about twenty minutes.

After I put the phone down, I got to thinking...

Whaaat? Remains? Well... Would they be ashes, and would they be in my driveway overnight? Then it occurred to me – if they were coming from a hospital then the 'remains' would not yet be ashes! The thought of a coffin in my driveway was something else entirely! Apart from me the other guests would not be too happy!

Well, eleven p.m. came and went and I was so tired and angry that by this time I was seriously considering telling the mother to tell them I was now closed and tell them to go to a hotel.

At that moment a car appeared and drove slowly into the driveway. I could see it was a long dark car but could not make out whether it was a hearse or not.

They were here now and so after receiving no apology for their lateness (apology for the pun!) I showed them quickly to their rooms and retired for the night having arranged with them for breakfast at eight thirty a.m.

Next morning, I saw that thankfully the vehicle was not a hearse but still it was an estate car with blacked out windows. Whatever was inside could not be seen by other guests. Thank goodness for that!

They arrived for breakfast dressed casually thank goodness however, time wise, these guys hadn't a clue as despite arranging breakfast for eight thirty a.m. they came in half an hour early and so had to sit at the table with other guests eating and wait till theirs was cooked. I just hoped they did not talk about what they did for a living! I tried listening behind the door, but it seemed they were talking about the weather and where they lived in Ireland.

When they were leaving, I finally asked about the 'remains' and was told that no, they had been delivered last night (wasn't going to Northern Ireland after all then).

Phew! This is what happens when you don't get the whole story at the beginning and the booking is done through a third party. Especially too when it is late at night and your mind is tired and you are trying to make sense of everything.

Chapter 5

<u>Filipinos</u>

Wow – another first.

This is what keeps me in the business of B&B! You just never know who is coming through the door.

This email booking was from a family who asked if I could take seven people for two nights – two small children plus five adults. OK, no problem, two adults plus two children in the family room and three adults in the twin and single room. Their address was Bedford in England, and the surname was a little unusual, but you get used to that.

Anyway, this family said they would arrive quite late as they had a long drive up from Bedford and would arrive around six p.m.

That afternoon, I was at my rental apartment getting it ready for guests but I was home in good time, as I thought, by being there at four p.m. Oh no, they've arrived and are all over the garden where my gardener had told them I would not be far away. They said it had taken them a shorter time to drive from Edinburgh and so they were much earlier. What? Edinburgh? I thought they said they were coming from Bedford?

Oh well don't ask and just accept. It turned out they were over from the Philippines touring on holiday. Mum Jane, Dad

Noli, son Julio, baby Yan-Yan, Auntie Christie, Grandad Connie (?) and Grandma Susan. All the adults spoke good English except Grandad Connie who just grunted. They were lovely people. The five-year-old, Julio, was very inquisitive and wanted to roam over the whole house to explore and had to be told some areas were private. I had been asked by email if cooking facilities were available and I told them that they could use the microwave to heat up the baby's milk but that my kitchen was not available as there were many excellent restaurants nearby. That was fine.

On arrival they had all taken off their shoes at the front door which was nice but then they began to take over the place!

They asked again if cooking facilities were available, and I said I don't usually do that but just for a couple of days I could. Then they said they had a camping stove. Father Noli proceeded to set up a wok on a camping stove on my patio making rice, meat and even sausages for the five-year-old Julio! I must say the smell of cooking was making me hungry! It was fascinating to see this guy hunkering down on the ground over a camping stove making dinner for six in a single wok. I have to admit it smelled good. He actually had enough food for six people in that large wok. While this was going on the mother was changing the baby's nappy on my leather couch! No changing mat, no "Is this all right?" or "Would you mind?" or "Where can I change a nappy?" The grandmother now is bringing through the full coffee cups from the bedrooms. She also lays out the paper plates and plastic cutlery on my dining table which is half set for the breakfast. Again, no "Can we do this?" It seems they think this is self-catering yet they gave me their orders for breakfast. I half expected to be asked for rice and noodles! No, six x Full Scottish breakfasts – I wondered if they would eat it! After their evening meal they tidied everything away beautifully and even put their trash in the correct re-cycling bins. Then they went off to see the town. They returned quite early around eight p.m. and proceeded to make themselves very much at home. They took over my lounge again and I busied myself in the kitchen where I felt I would rather catch up on chores than talk to six adults plus a baby. Not that I'm not good at that but at that time of night I felt it a little overwhelming not to mention noisy. On one of my visits to the lounge (just to check all was well not only for them but for me too) I was asked by the mother what I was doing in the kitchen.

"Oh, there are always many things to keep me busy…" I didn't tell her I was writing about them!

They went to bed around ten p.m. (perhaps the fact I was re-setting the breakfast table was a hint!) I noticed that they had drawn the curtains at the end of the room? Again, no "Can we do this?"

As I went up to bed, I saw that they had drawn the hall curtains at the front door too. Were they cold?

They had ordered breakfast for nine a.m. At eight a.m. I heard them down in the lounge. I dressed quickly and asked them if they would like to eat earlier? Yes, eight thirty would be fine. They all came to the table at different times and so I was serving non-stop for a while. Father was first to be served and he said, "Is this my breakfast?"

"Yes," I said wondering what he was meaning. I think they had not done B&B before and maybe he was wondering if it was to share or all for him.

The five-year-old, Julio, was having frosted flakes and when he didn't finish them (do young children ever clean their plates?) his dad emptied it complete with all the milk into his own bowl.

"I hate to waste food," he said. Maybe he thought that his breakfast was not enough, but some people think it is large!

Every member of the family ate a large bowl of cereal then all the cooked breakfast and all the toast. I wondered whether they thought it might be rude to leave any as is the custom in Japan. Well, they won't need any lunch!

When they were finished, I asked them if they would like to try haggis and/or black pudding the next day.

"Yes," they all said. On asking which they would like they said, "Both!" OK...

I asked about the drawing of the curtains and mother said it was so that the neighbours didn't see in. Because of the trees this is not possible and as for the hall at the front door the glass is frosted glass and we have a large garden fringed with more trees! OK...

After breakfast while the family were preparing for the day's activities, I found that the TV was on, and the youngster was enjoying cartoons. Now my TV is not easy to put on unless you know how to use the different remotes and adjust the batteries in one of them. OK... Somebody must be very 'techy' minded.

Perhaps you may be thinking I should have said that this is not self-catering but B&B only. I could, but what harm are they doing, and they are only here for two nights. Give them a good impression of the Scots and Ayrshire, and they were very pleasant.

The next night they were so tired after the day's outing that they didn't sit in the lounge other than to tell me of their day. Little Julio had got bored and said, "I want to go back to Margaret's house!"

Bless...

The next breakfast was also all eaten apart from a couple of slices of black pudding.

Before leaving they wanted to photograph me with them, and I took pictures of them in the garden for them. Then they gave me a bank note from the Philippines for my collection of international currencies on the wall in the lounge telling me that the one I had was now obsolete so here was a new one. Now I can tell you that the currency in the Philippines is the Peso!

The car they were driving was not large and I wondered how on earth they were going to get everything in. Seven people, a baby seat, a child seat, bags and picnic bags. It took two people to pile everything up in the tiny boot space then one person to hold the bags from inside to stop them falling out when the boot was opened! The car moved off with the suspension very near the ground!

All's well – who will come in next?

Chapter 6

Strange People

This is another wedding tale but a rather different one.

A booking came in for two single rooms for a couple coming for a wedding. Apparently, there was a snoring problem! On the night of their arrival, they telephoned to say they were on the train. Just after that their son arrived with their wedding outfits, dropped them off, then left. (Why didn't he pick them up from the station?) Within ten minutes of him leaving they arrived from the station by taxi. Mother was Chinese and father, a Londoner, dressed in a track suit and both had back packs! Mother was very sharp tongued and did not act like she was part of a happy wedding party at all. Father was smelling strongly of smoke but apologised as ours is a non-smoking house. He then went for a walk, presumably to light up again. Later the son came back but there were no hugs or family greetings – not even a smile. Mother left them soon after and went to her room. The son, when leaving, had to knock on her door to say a brief goodbye. At breakfast father mentioned the smoke again and said that they had been in a very smoky train, and it was their clothes which smelt, not them. Yeah right!

Well, could be but when people have been smoking their breath smells for some time after.

When I was doing room service for them later, I saw that the mother had slept in a bag on top of a larger bag and had a pillow roll – all on top of the made bed.

They came back early from the wedding obviously not being party people! The next morning, they were offered a lift to the station by the other wedding guests and the father gladly accepted but the mother changed his mind in order not to inconvenience them – which it didn't!

Oh well, at least I didn't have to change her bed! She must have barely moved!

Wuxing – no, not waxing – wuxing!

I think this is more unusual than strange – well maybe a bit strange too!

A number of years ago a mother booked in for herself and her daughter in two rooms for one night. They were meeting up after being apart for several years in different countries. The daughter had late-stage cancer and was on her way to Germany for treatment. She arrived later than her mother and she was wearing a pretty snood on her head to disguise the fact she had no hair, presumably the result of chemotherapy. She explained her situation and said she had a special request to ask me.

"OK," I said, full of sympathy. She told me that she was studying alternative therapies, the current one being the Chinese Cosmic cycles of "Wuxing," known as the five elements of Earth, Water, Fire, Metal and Wood. I did not know anything about this but listened to her explanation. It seemed very complicated, but I can fully understand that with such a desperate diagnosis such as hers you would be willing to try anything and so her story was anything but funny.

The question she asked me was, "Would it be possible for me to light a fire in the back garden and sleep there beside it?"

Wow I wasn't expecting that! I thought about this request for a bit then said, "I'm really sorry but there is nowhere suitable in the garden and the neighbours would be upset seeing there was a fire next door. Overnight, if they saw the flames, they might call the fire brigade being afraid it would spread to the trees then over the fence to them." She was quite upset at this refusal so eventually I suggested she sleep in the lounge with the gas fire on low. I checked with her mother about this, and she said her daughter had done this before and that she doesn't move in her sleeping bag and so is quite safe.

So, that night she brought down her sleeping bag and placed it perpendicularly to the fireplace (this being essential apparently) and this is when I saw that she indeed had no hair.

I did worry through the night and at about three p.m. I crept halfway down the stairs and peeped through the internal window into the lounge and sure enough she had not moved from her strategically placed pencil shaped sleeping bag. She was at right angles to the hearth with her head almost touching the tiles and with no protection of the pillow or cushion which I had offered.

In the morning I came down into the lounge on route to the kitchen ready to prepare breakfasts. I was surprised (again!) to see that she was now sitting ON the hearth (fire still on!) with crossed legs in the lotus position with her arms bent up and her thumbs and first fingers touching. She was silent and seemed to be in a trance. Oh dear, I had other guests coming down for breakfast in forty-five minutes and she would have to move! I said her name softly hoping not to startle her from her trance. I repeated that a few times a little more loudly. There was still no response. I then started the breakfast preparations rattling cups and shutting cupboard doors loudly etc. and even tried whistling but to no avail. Eventually with just ten minutes to go I had to try again. I put my hand on her shoulder and shook her gently speaking her name. She came out of it thank goodness and slowly managed to hear what I was saying and agreed to go upstairs. I put the fire off and managed to have a normal breakfast time! The other guests had no idea there had been anything unusual going on overnight!

Mother and daughter left after their breakfast (blueberries and natural yoghurt only for the daughter), and I never heard how the German treatment worked for her. I would love to think she recovered.

The Miseries

Oh dear, with some people you don't know whether to feel sorry for them or be irritated!

This couple were booked in by their son who lived locally. He had called a couple of times about the booking and, at first, I thought he sounded elderly. His voice was very low and hesitant as if he was in advanced stages of depression.

"Heavens," I thought, I hope the parents are not like that.

They were booked in for four nights which normally would be a bonus but, in this case, I wasn't so sure.

On the day of their arrival, they were due in around seven to eight p.m. At nine forty-five p.m. the son called to say that father was ill and so they would not be coming that night if at all but that he would call in the morning to let me know if they would be staying that night.

The next morning, having heard nothing, I called him around ten thirty a.m. to see how he was. Yes, father was better, and he thought they were coming.

"They're not up yet, hold on and I'll ask them..."

Not up at ten thirty a.m.? Elderly people are usually up and about early.

He came back to say yes, they would be coming.

"What time?" I asked.

"Oh... evening, I think."

Well, as with a lot of people who say a time, that didn't happen. They turned up mid-afternoon (luckily, I was in) and the son came to the door leaving them still in the car. The son looked exactly like he sounded, dull, grey, and miserable. When the parents came in, I saw immediately where the son got his demeanour from! A more miserable looking pair you couldn't imagine! The son brought in the one suitcase, yet they had booked two rooms. The contents of the suitcase would have to be carried back and forth between the rooms.

I always worry if I have very elderly people staying especially if they are upstairs which is where my single rooms are.

They climbed slowly up and got settled in and after having a rest the son would return at around six p.m. in order to take them for a meal. I noticed that after taking the suitcase upstairs the son just left without even a 'see you later'. OK...

Son duly returned at six p.m. and off they went to return

at ten p.m. Breakfast was ordered for nine a.m.

They came down (phew they survived the night!) and sat at the table. Mother always looked disapproving of everything, but I don't think she was, it was just her manner. I asked them if they had slept well, and father said yes. Mother, however, said she'd had nightmares and wakened up but had gone to sleep again.

"Oh dear, oh good," I said.

Then she said she had hurt her back in the bathroom. She had stood up and it just happened.

"Oh dear…"

She seemed to be moving as well as before thankfully.

Having served them porridge and mother having sausage and egg I sat in the kitchen with my cuppa. I heard a noise which made me look up but didn't hear anything else. Then I heard, "Hello, hello…"

Oh, oh, what's happened?

I went through to see and there was a scene of devastation! Father had knocked over his full cafetiere, broken it, coffee all over the table, the carpet and his trousers! Luckily, he did not burn himself or his wife. I mopped up as best I could (not his trousers!) and made him more coffee. I noticed that there were no apologies forthcoming.

"He's usually so careful," said mother who, now, I noticed, was shaking as with Parkinson's.

Now I know why they were not staying with their son.

Once they had gone out for the day (collected by still morose son) I went to do the usual room service. Both rooms had a plastic bag on the floor full of medications. There were also packets on the tables. No wonder they were barely moving – they were drugged to the eyeballs! The next thing I noticed was that there was a nightdress on the unmade bed. This was the father's room – they must have changed rooms? Fair enough, one room is through the wall from the bathroom and so maybe they realised they needed to swap. Then I moved along to the other room. There was another nightdress on that bed! Maybe it was a night-shirt? No, they were both long, flannelette, and covered with small flowers!

In the course of conversation (which only really consisted of me making small talk and them answering in one sentence), father told me they had driven up from Guildford to Nottingham before they discovered they had left their medication behind. They had gone all the way back then come up by plane! Maybe they had forgotten his pyjamas as well and so he had borrowed mother's nightdress if she had brought two?

They stayed the four nights and each night when they came in it was a case of "We ate at…" or "We went to…"

"Did you enjoy that?" I would ask.

"Yes."

One night it was "We played cards."

"Oh, that was nice," I said. I had given up trying to have a conversation by then.

Each morning there was never a 'Good morning' to mine, just "I had nightmares again" from mother (some tablets can do this too!), or father "I had hiccups in the night."

"Oh dear…"

"I drink out of the wrong side of the glass, have you heard of that one?"

"Yes," I said, "did it work?"

"Yes."

"Oh good…" Yeah a conversation!

On leaving they actually smiled and said what a good time they had had. I'm glad and pleased for them.

Poltergeist

A nice couple from Ireland arrived and it was soon apparent that the wife was rather a hyper type and would not stop talking! We were still at the 'Here is your room and what would you like for breakfast' stage when I became aware that I was leaning from one foot to the other and saying long lists of "Really?", "Oh dear", "What a shame", "Yes", "No" etc. in response to her chatter while her husband just stood there. When I managed to escape, I was thinking how glad I was that they were only staying for one night!

In the morning, she started again, and while I was listening to her their breakfast got frazzled and I just apologised and said, "I must have been talking too much!"

When they were ready to leave, she came into the lounge and said, "Do you have a poltergeist in that bedroom?"

"Pardon?" My eyebrows had risen – was she serious?

"Well, you must have, because, neither my husband nor myself could find the toothpaste." I could see she was perfectly serious and not joking.

"Oh," I said, trying not to smile, and not succeeding at all. "Not that I know of anyway."

"Has no one ever said that before?" she continued.

"No…"

"Well, I'm sure there is because we saw the toothpaste last night, then it disappeared, but I thought oh well I'll leave my teeth till the morning, then it wasn't there again, and we both searched high and low. It's the angels you know, they do it for a reason…"

"Well," I said, "I wonder why they would hide your toothpaste!"

Ignoring that she went on," It's the same with watches (?), I don't wear expensive watches as I just lose them. It's the angels telling me to slow down (well it's not working, is it?). I'm all up tight and I know it (!), my mother has dementia, my husband's out of work, the cat's not well…"

"Oh dear," I sympathised (oh dear I'm doing it again!).

Next, she gazed round my walls and said, "You're well protected here – you've got an owl, the pharaoh lamp – she's looking after you." (She? Well, there were a few female pharaohs, but my lamp was definitely male.)

"Oh good," I said, "I'm glad to hear that."

"And," she continued, "I like the face (a wooden face plaque holiday souvenir), that's good."

Her husband, bless him, took her away saying, "We must let Margaret get on…"

After they'd gone, I went into their room and thought, "Well, if the toothpaste is here, I'll find it."

Sure enough, I found it. It had been put in the plastic cup on the wash basin behind the face flannel which was folded into a fan shape.

The next day I had a telephone message waiting for me from that couple saying they had taken the room key by mistake and would post it back to me. I wanted to know what she would say when I told her the toothpaste was found and so I phoned them back and said I had found it.

"Oh, where was it?" she cried. When I told her she said, "Oh, it must have been the fairies, they do that you know…"

Course they do!

Chapter 7

Reiki

Reiki practitioners would not call themselves strange people either then or now but at the time of their visit Reiki was little known as an alternative health treatment.

I received a booking from a self-professed Reiki 'Master' who was coming with her 'protégé'. This should be interesting as I did not know much about Reiki. Having learnt not to question people for fear of giving the wrong (or right!) impression I booked them in. On arrival the two ladies came in with a tremendous amount of paraphernalia, in addition to the usual bags, cases etc. They had large plastic baskets full of assorted balls and toys and two large folding treatment tables.

The 'Master' was here to conduct a four-day course for Reiki Students. The cost of this to the students was several hundred pounds as I saw from the documents they had. Quite a lucrative employment even back then! I was given a brochure and saw that Reiki is a healing hands treatment to relieve stress and anxiety and miscellaneous illnesses. No touching of the body occurs.

Being the great sceptic I am, of all alternative, hypnotic or yoga type treatments I was not overly impressed. Not that I would deny for a minute that alternative treatments can help many people where traditional treatments have failed. I am not one to rush to indulge but I'm sure that if I had tried everything else and not found a cure for something then I would certainly try anything. I had tried hypnosis when much younger but that is another story!

During their four-day stay, while I was doing room service, I saw some interesting things. Over the radiator was hung a bikini outfit the top part of which was made out of real coconuts with dozens of little metal medallions attached to it. The bottom part was a grass skirt. (What kind of treatment was this then?) I didn't ask! On the bedside table was a box of 'Hopi Ear Candles'? I just had to look at that! Apparently, this was a treatment for ear wax and tinnitus. The patient lies on their side with the candle inserted into the ear then it is set fire to! No, really! There was a picture of this on the box with the patient lying on their side with a flaming straw stuck in their ear! I thought, "I don't believe this!" Since then, I have discovered that ear candles have become quite popular and a well-known treatment. Next, I couldn't help noticing that both ladies had their own bag full of homeopathic and herbal medicines. Why, I wondered, if their treatment was so wonderful, why would they need them?

The Reiki 'Master' stayed regularly for three years with different 'protégés' one of which was memorable for the fact that she had waist length hair and wore horn necklaces and quartz rings said to have medicinal properties.

One of the years three young girls came and they were taking the course. We got talking, as you do, and they said they needed to practise, and would I like a session? Well, my health certainly needed an energy boost and so I thought, "Why not?" You can't judge if you haven't tried it.

They had me lie down on top of the bed and covered me with a duvet (to be covered I thought was strange), and all three girls worked on me. One was at my legs, one in the middle, and one behind my head. I was told to relax with my eyes shut and they would convey energy from them to me. If only! I lay there for half an hour trying not to laugh or even smile. They didn't say anything during the treatment, but now and again made a mmmm humming sound.

At the end of the session one of the girls (the one in the middle) said she had never felt so drained and that I was pulling in energy like nobody's business. She was hot and perspiring. Well, I thought, I don't know where the energy was going but it certainly wasn't going into me! Wish that it had! Maybe it got stuck in the duvet!

"Thank you," I said. "I really enjoyed the restful treatment and I'm sure it has done me a power of good."

Yoga

One family had a son who was about nineteen years old, and he did yoga. My daughter came to me one afternoon and said, "Mum, there's someone meditating in the back garden!"

"What?"

I went to look and sure enough at the end of the house on the grass was the son sitting in the lotus position with his hands on his knees and the pointer fingers on the thumbs. His eyes were closed, and he was making a repetitive humming sound. Oh well…

Hypnosis

This is just to explain why I have yet to be convinced of the efficacy of some kinds of alternative medicine. I do believe that if you believe it will work then it has a good chance. I try, I really do!

So, this is my tale of my one and only hypnosis treatment.

When I was young, I suffered very badly from asthma and lost many school and working days because of it. I tried many treatments including homeopathic, allergy injections, and cortisone treatment with bad side effects.

In my early twenties my GP had just taken a course in hypnosis and wondered if I would like to be a guinea pig for him. Well, if you don't try it...

I was to go after work when his surgery was finished (he would not be allowed to do this nowadays, but then it was not a problem).

He welcomed me in and lifted the phone to tell his receptionist he didn't want to be disturbed for the next half hour. (Again, he could not do this now and it also made me feel quite uncomfortable.) He had me lie on the treatment table and pulled a stool right up almost touching the table. This unnerved me right away and I instinctively moved over nearer the wall! I had my ankles crossed and was told to uncross them, hands by my side. Not conducive to relaxing I can tell you! Then he took out a ball point pen and held it above my face (not a swinging pendulum but it might as well have been!). I laughed nervously and he kept telling me to relax! I kept thinking of the stereotype hypnotists on TV. His first mistake was to put on a 'hypnotist's voice' – monotone and very slow. I burst out laughing again and almost said 'You cannot be serious!' But he was... "Sorry, sorry," I said, "I'll try harder..."

He started again and I bit my bottom lip hard in order not to laugh. Eventually I couldn't keep it in any longer and laughed again. "Sorry, sorry."

"Just relax, and we'll start again…"

Trying really hard I got past the introductory bit and then I was told that I was feeling nice and warm and comfortable, "Actually," I said, "my feet are very cold. My feet are always cold." He sighed and went to get me a blanket for my feet then started again. He got to the warm and comfortable bit again and kept repeating that slowly, "Warm and comfortable", "Warm and comfortable". And I then thought, *If he keeps repeating that any longer, he is going to say 'corm and womfortable!'* This made me crack up hugely and I had to apologise again.

"Deep breaths and just relax and let yourself go." Right. Trying so hard with a bruised lip I got to the bit where he said my left arm was feeling very light, VERY light, and is rising off the bed into the air. At that point a really strange thing happened – my arm did the very opposite and actually felt that it was pushing down on the bed!

It was then I realised my brain had no intention of being taken over by anyone! Hypnosis was not for me, however much I wished it to work. You may be interested to know that after that my GP gave up his foray into hypnosis and it never came on to his list of skills!

This Is Someone Who Really Needed to Relax!

An English retired couple arrived and although it was to be only one night it seemed so much longer! She was a nonstop talker and question asker. "Have you children? Where are they? Are they now married? Do your husband and children play golf? Where do YOU go on holiday? When? How long for? How many rooms do you have? Are you full now?"

Then she gave her life story as husband stayed silent. She told of him having stenosis of the spine and so can't sit for long. SHE has tablets to take... All this is normal type stuff but... not whilst you are still showing them to their room!

The next morning, I was finishing the laying of milk, butter etc. on the table, when she came through and started again, the minute she saw me. She was looking at my photos of the children.

Like most people I have photographs of my family on the wall in my living room and so this started her off. I have three university graduation photographs of my children and some wedding pictures too. She asked me what they were all studying and where are they now and do I have any grandchildren? I told her that two of my children live abroad in the USA and Australia and so I have to contact them via Skype and Face Time and what would we do without these devices? I introduced these subjects in order to head her off asking about the third picture of my oldest son. He died when he was twenty-five years old from a heart problem diagnosed at the age of seven. I had taken my younger son who was five years old to the doctor as he had developed a fever. The older boy was along too and so the doctor checked him too. He seemed to take a longer time than usual in listening to his chest and when he had finished, he looked at me over his glasses and said, "Did you know this child has a heart murmur?"

"No," I said, horrified.

I came out of the surgery with my arms round my boys, one with scarlet fever and the other with a heart murmur.

At the hospital they said his heart was beating very slowly and that he would need a pacemaker, but they could not fit one until his chest was large enough to accommodate one. This was done when he was fifteen. He never had any symptoms and led a completely normal life. He started up his own computer business and was doing really well and had such a bright future before him. He lived in London with his girlfriend and had no reason to worry about his health as he had been told that he, with the pacemaker, should have a perfectly normal life span. Unfortunately, his pacemaker, unlike the ones now, was only programmed to stop the heart beating too slowly and could not stop it going too fast. This, unfortunately, was what happened.

Sometimes my strategy in diverting the conversation worked but quite often I was asked 'And the third one?' Then I would have to quickly decide whether to tell people or just say, 'Well happily he is more local, being in London.' If I tell them then they are so sorry and wish they hadn't asked and if I say London, then I usually ask them questions about their family to head them off. I don't like saying either of these options and I've often thought I should take down his picture, but I would feel that I would be removing him from my life. A thing I don't want to do.

She, of course, asked about the third one and I told her that he was in London so that was much better and then I asked her about her family, and she told of hers. At an appropriate moment in her story (really when she took a breath!) I said, "That's great, well, do help yourselves to the cereals etc. and I'll get cracking with your breakfast." (No pun intended!)

On leaving she told me she wished she could go to the loo but can't! She has problems that way! WAY too much information! That explains the box of toilet seat covers she was carrying when she arrived then!

Chapter 8

Chess Chumps

Sometimes we tend to categorise people according to their job, name, hobbies etc. Well, people who play chess can sometimes be perceived as rather geeky (as are computer buffs). Of course, this is a complete generalisation, but there is some truth to it.

In our town there is an annual chess championship which lasts all week with a different competition held at the weekend. For the week's championship I had three single men, two older ones who could have qualified for the senior competition but elected to play in the bottom grade tournament as they felt that the senior one was too difficult! They came on their own and each one I would say was a 'right old woman' the way they talked about anything and everything. I was glad to leave them to talk at each other (you notice I said 'at' and not 'to') at the breakfast table, to the point where I had to suggest to them that when they were finished eating, they would be more comfortable moving to the lounge? (I had more people due to arrive for breakfast at any moment.) The third man was younger and hardly said a word to me at any time and was a bit outflanked by the other two.

For the weekend tournament a father and son arrived on

the doorstep. Almost before they said hello the father was complaining about the long walk from the station. (One mile!) Too mean to take a taxi? The son (the chess player) was just standing saying nothing. I offered to try to find them somewhere nearer the town centre but after futile phone calls they had to stay put. Over the weekend I would give them a lift in my car when I could. While I was asking for their breakfast choices, I noticed that the son (who was about thirty years of age) was rocking back and forth constantly. Oh dear, I thought, that is why dad has to travel with him. They had a slow discussion about breakfast times and when the chess started. After looking up his papers for the tournament it still wasn't clear to me whether it was ten a.m. or noon! Anyway, they plumped for breakfast at eight thirty a.m.

"And what would you like from the menu?"

"I'll have the cooked," said the dad, "just toast for the son."

"Tea? coffee?"

"Tea," said the dad.

"Yes," said the son.

"You could have coffee if you want," said the dad.

"No, I'll have tea." He's still rocking.

"What's your name?" the dad asked me.

"Margaret," I said. (I'd told them that when they arrived – although I forget names as soon as said too but then I have too many to remember – they only had one!)

"Margaret," says the dad, "I have seven sisters…" and he started pointing at his fingers and naming them in his head. "No, I don't think there's a Margaret…"

Doesn't he know if he has a sister called Margaret? It should be a fun weekend then.

They had only been in about half an hour when the dad came down and gave me two cheques in different names. "That's my name," he said pointing to one signature, "and Ben, (the son) is Brown." He changed his name by deed poll years ago." I didn't ask!

The next morning, they were sharing a table with two other people and when I went in with the teas, I saw that the son was staring down at the table cover. Father talked to the others, but the son said nothing. I felt sorry for both of them as there was definitely a medical problem there. The following day one of the others was leaving and he said, "Has that guy ever spoken?"

The son, however, was very good at chess and won several of his games. I do think he had a health problem, so it was not his fault he was a little unusual.

One of the other players was chatty but only about his own little world. After the first day he had been beaten and he was annoyed to discover he's been drawn against a previous champion! The next day he came back raging again because he had been beaten again and this time by an eleven-year-old girl! It turned out she was a junior champion! He was so mad he had gone to the organisers to complain about his doubly unlucky draws. I don't think he got anywhere with that!

Strange Names

Occasionally we get phone calls from people, usually in pubs, who phone and make bookings in strange names just for a laugh. Indeed there are many people with unusual names and so you have to accept every name which is said just in case it is genuine. I learned this early on as I had received a phone call from a woman whose name was Brenda Ramsbottom and I was convinced it was a friend of mine's voice making a joke and I had replied, "Aye right, and how many weeks would you like to stay?"

"Pardon?" came the voice and then I realised she was real!

On a visit into the next town this day I happened to drop into the tourist information centre to drop in some local leaflets of my town and while I was there, I gave my availability for the weekend. I returned an hour later as I had forgotten to collect some golf leaflets and there were two men at the desk looking for accommodation for three nights for the Scottish Grand National which was on that weekend. They were being told that the town was full. I stepped in and said that The Cherries had a couple of rooms, and could I help? I explained that we were only eight miles from the racecourse and just fifteen minutes by car. The assistant then passed them over to me and I now had a sizeable booking! For directions to my place, I said if they followed me, I would take them there. Happily, we all set off and they followed in their car. Driving home I was thinking, "What am I doing – I have just picked up two strange men and am taking them to my home!"

On arrival I asked them to sign the Visitors' Book with their names and addresses. They did that and then dropped their bags in their room then went off to have a look round the town. I checked the book and was astounded to see that one of them was named, "Pickup!" I swear on my life this was his real name!

You Cannot Be Serious

Another call was from someone who sounded like he was phoning on a mobile phone in a pub or a car as his voice kept cutting out. He managed to ask for a double room for that night.

"Yes, that's fine," I said. "What's your name?"

"Barney," was all he said and then the line went dead again.

A few minutes later he called again saying he was on the boat coming into Oban (a good three hours away) and so they would arrive around nine p.m. Ah, I thought, that is why the phone kept cutting out, he was on a boat! I then asked his name again.

"Barney," he said again.

"And your last name?" I asked again.

"I'll spell it for you," he said. "F-a-w-c-u-f." Of course, I didn't try to pronounce it! I thought to myself, this HAS to be a wind up! I looked up all the phone books in the house to see if such a name existed. Not one was listed.

However, about eight thirty p.m., the doorbell rang and there they were – a perfectly nice-looking couple. Neither they nor I mentioned their name. I was determined to get their name in writing and as most B&Bs do not have registration forms in the morning I said to them, "Would you like to sign the Visitors' Book? I should have asked you last night."

Often, I forget to ask people to sign the book as I am so busy welcoming them and they don't usually ask if they have to sign in.

"Certainly," he said.

When they left, I went to look at their entry and, disappointedly, they had only written 'Barney and Sheila' (ah, pity, but no wonder!) and their address! How can anyone possibly live with a name like that? Imagine the poor girl who would marry into that name never mind the best man's speech at the wedding!

Chapter 9

<u>For This One Make Up Your Own Mind!</u>

As I've said many times, "There's nowt so strange as folk."

If this phone call had come at night, I would definitely say the man was phoning from a pub with his mates for a laugh.

He actually sounded genuine and not drunk at all and it was happening at around lunch time. He had a strong Irish accent.

"Is that the guest house?"

"Yes, it is. This is The Cherries."

"A wee bird told me that you have an up-market place – is that right?"

"Yes, indeed and who was it telling you that?" (I'm already copying his accent instinctively. My daughter says she always knows the nationality of whoever I'm speaking to on the phone. I don't mean to do it, it just happens.)

"Oh, word of mouth, word of mouth,"

"When would you like to stay?"

"I don't have the exact dates yet, I just want to find out about your place. Is it a good area?"

"Oh yes, very quiet and residential."

"That's grand, that's grand – how far is it to the town and the beach?"

"About one and a half miles."

"Do you offer transport; I won't have a car?"

"Well, if I'm going out, I am happy to drop you off in the town."

"That's very kind of you so it is. Do you have a bath? I like a bath."

"Yes, it is a full ensuite."

"That's lovely, now, do you have towels?"

"Oh yes, and a hospitality tray and TV in the room."

"Wonderful, do you have green towels?"

"You're winding me up now."

"No, no, I like a green towel, I'm very patriotic. Should I phone back nearer the time then, would that be the thing to do?"

"Yes, that would be fine."

"I'll be with my three birds."

Does he mean three daughters? Girlfriends? Is that the way he speaks of them?

"How old are they?"

"Ehhh, six years, eighteen months and six months."

"Well, I can give you the family room ensuite with a double bed and a single bed and do you have a travel cot?"

"Just the cages."

"Pardon?"

"The cages – for the birds."

"Real birds?"

"Yes, I have an eagle and an albatross and an Osprey."

"Now you are really winding me up!"

"No, no, I have to say that it puts people off when I tell them about the birds, but they are very well behaved and come everywhere with me."

"Well, I think they wouldn't do well with my cats."

"Do you have cats?"

"Yes."

"Oh well that wouldn't do then. They couldn't stay where there are cats."

"Well, I hope you find somewhere suitable. Sorry I can't think of anywhere I can suggest. Maybe a hotel could help."

"I'll try that, you've been very helpful yourself. You have a great day now."

"Goodbye now."

That phone call was my laugh for the day!

Odd Balls

Oddballs are actually quite common. In fact, this book was inspired by them.

Single visitors fall into this category most often – most likely that is why they are on their own!

This one arrived for four nights. On reaching his room he said straight away and very seriously, "I'll pay you now as I wouldn't like to get mugged (what here?) – I've never been mugged but you never know." Then he gave me the money and to make sure that I didn't think he was giving me a tip as he said, "I'll give you this and you can give me the two pounds." (Yes sir!)

Within the next five minutes he had asked me who else was staying at the time then told me he hated barking dogs, and noisy children, loud people and people he couldn't understand. He confessed he was a bit of a loner. I assured him that none of these categories were staying and just hoped that none arrived before he left. Luckily none did. He wanted sausage and bacon for breakfast and very strong tea.

"Please don't give me tomato – I have stayed at many B&Bs, and you wouldn't believe how many people give me tomato when I ask for sausage and bacon."

"No, I won't then." (I wasn't going to anyway!)

"How do you like your sausage and bacon?" I asked before he could tell me.

"Sausage, browned on both sides and very crispy bacon but not burnt."

"I'll do my best." At this there was no smile or acknowledgement, so I left him to it.

After a while he left to check out the area and took from his car one of those bicycles which has the miniscule wheels and very high saddles. Off he trundled. I had to smile at the sight.

At the breakfast table next morning he placed a box of medications in front of him and proceeded to count out the day's allocation. I am amazed at the number of people who do this – why not take them before or after the meal and in private? They don't have to be taken while you are actually eating! (Some people will ask me for a glass of water to take them with and then proceed to tell me all their symptoms!)

I brought in his strong tea and when I brought in his sausage and bacon, I noticed he had covered the tea pot in… a black woolly hat! No, not a tea cosy, a black woolly hat! That really made me laugh! (Not in front of him!) Maybe I should have said, "What a great idea, do you carry that everywhere? But that might have produced a comment about the failings of B&Bs!

On clearing his plates away, I noticed that there were three tea bags in the single size tea pot. I'm sure I hadn't put three in, two yes, but not three. Oh well, he'll get three tomorrow. Did he add another the next morning? No, so he must have checked.

There was no complaint regarding the sausage and bacon so I reckoned that they must have passed muster!

Harry the Walker – Another O. B.

I was phoned by the Girvan tourist information centre (TIC) for one single room for one night. Name of, "I'll spell it for you," she said, obviously grinning. (Yes, another one!) "H-j-e-l-m-s-t-a-d," she said, "with the J not sounded and the D pronounced as a T."

"OK, no problem." I smiled.

"He will arrive at eight p.m."

Actually, it was ten minutes past nine when he came. No apology. On greeting him I said his name with a 'T' and asked if that was correct.

"Nearly," he said, but did not say what it was. He walks thirty miles a day. I had warned the TIC that the nearest restaurant was a twenty-minute walk from here but he was not fussed as he was a walker. Fine. I had just thought after thirty miles he would not have wanted to walk any more that night. It had been a wet day and his clothes and shoes were wet and I offered to put them in the drying room for him. He acted as if this was expected. I then asked him if he was going to go out to eat?

"Well, that depends," he said in his louder than average voice.

"I usually eat sandwiches at night but didn't pass anywhere (yes he must have!) and so could you make me a couple of rounds with cheese, tomato, and some butter?"

What could I say to such a specific request?

"Do I have a tea pot here?" he asked.

"Yes, there is one on your tray," I indicated.

"Could I have a larger one, I need to drink after the walking."

"Yes, of course," I said.

"Just when you're ready," he said.

"For breakfast I will have two sausages, two eggs and tomato cut into two pieces, tea and toast. I like to have these things organised before so there is no confusion."

"Very good," I said. "How would you like your eggs?" and waited for the details.

"Both turned over, not soft, so that I can hold them."

"Right," I said and went to finish my interrupted TV programme.

I made him two toasted cheese and tomato rolls with a salad garnish and took him his larger tea pot.

I knocked on his door and heard, "Just leave it at the door, I am not so respectable." You're right, I thought. No 'thank you' came through the door.

In the morning he sat at the table and said, "I will have what I said last night and bring the tea and toast after."

Didn't his English lessons include the words 'Please' and 'Thank you'? These are usually the first words you learn in any language.

Doing 'the chat' I asked him how long he was here to walk and where was he heading?

"Till 2 Oct at four p.m. John O' Groats I finish." OK…

"When did you start?"

"8 June at ten a.m. from Harwich. I like to be precise –

this annoys some people, but some people find it interesting."

Interesting maybe, but he can't be doing many miles per day if he was taking six months to go from Harwich to John O' Groats. Also, why did he start at Harwich? Maybe the ferry came in there, but he could have taken the train to Dover or even Land's End to walk the whole of Britain. I wasn't going to ask as his demeanour was not conducive to a friendly conversation!

Not once did he smile.

I went back to the kitchen thinking, I bet he's single! Now to be fair the guy was Swedish, and his English wasn't perfect, but neither was his manner! He was interesting though.

Another Walker

This was January. A young woman called to book into my self-catering apartment for three nights. Maybe visiting relatives as January is not really a vacation month? I accepted her booking and two days before entry a gentleman called to say that he was booked into the apt in two days' time, but he was in the area now and did I know any reasonably priced B&Bs nearby? Well, actually... He booked in with me and said he was at a town about sixty miles away and would phone when he was nearer to get directions.

"Can I give you a lift from the station?" I asked.

"No," he said, "I am not allowed to take public transport."

Had he been barred from trains/buses due to drunken/drug/violent behaviour maybe? He didn't sound like that sort of guy at all.

After I had spoken with him, I had a thought. I was actually going to the apartment that morning to do the changeover and so it occurred to me that I could have him go there for the same price and it would save him moving in in two days' time and it would save me doing another room here. I called him back, but his mobile was not answering and for some reason I couldn't leave a message.

It took me an hour longer than I expected to do the flat and when I returned there was a message from him on my landline saying he was about two miles away up a hill behind the town. If he was coming here, he would have been here a while ago. All I could do was to wait for him to call back as the number on his phone was again not answering. Why would he keep putting it off? Maybe it was to preserve battery life?

He did call. He was way past the house and down at the sea front where he said Google had directed him. Need to check that out!

As he was near the apartment, I told him of my suggestion, and he was glad to be going there and I said I would meet him there in five minutes. Did he have a backpack so that I would recognise him?

No, he was pulling a trolley. OK, I would find him easily.

Sure enough, he was standing outside the flat with a trolley. He was wearing a grey 'hoodie' so I couldn't see his face from the car. Hmmm...

I approached him and was glad to see that he had a nice face and smile and was very well spoken and 'respectable' even if he had obviously not shaved for a while! I said I was keen to hear his story and he said he would certainly tell me.

He left his trolley round the corner from the foot of the stairs and on reaching the top flat he was so very appreciative of how warm it was. He had camped out the night before in his tent beside a loch, and the temperature was several minus degrees. He said he'd never been as cold in his life! In the morning when he took out the tent poles the tent stood up by itself being frozen solid!

His story:

The reason he could not take public transport was that he was walking round the world for a cancer charity. He had started in September from the south of France (it was now the end of December!) had come north over the channel to do Land's End to John O' Groats then back down to Ireland. He had met a girl (the one who had booked the flat) on his travels and decided to take a break with her and arranged to meet her here. He had only met her once, briefly! She lived in England. Amazing how people find each other!

I had to ask him since he was walking round the world why would he be in a cold country in the winter and not arrange it so that he could at least camp in warm countries seasonally?

His answer was that he wanted to stretch himself as a challenge. I suspect he will be re-thinking that one!

His plan now was to do Ireland then stop for a while to raise much more money by sponsorship from big companies. The trip so far had cost him much more than he had expected and taken much longer than he thought it would.

He was a great guy and said that for a long time he had wanted to help people but didn't know how to do that. This idea took hold and he gave up his job, sold his house and car, and took to the road after long preparations. He estimated it would take him three years to complete. He did not have close family or friends who had cancer but knew many people who did with numbers growing every year. In fact, the girl he had met had had cancer herself and was clearly impressed with his mission. I wonder if they will stay together?

I hope he makes it and good luck to him.

I gave him a contribution and I really hope he completes his plans. He could then write a book about his travels and what happened to him along the way. He even has a love interest whether or not she stays with him!

Chapter 10

The Flower Club

There is a very active flower club in this town, and I hosted the demonstrators (so called as they demonstrate how to arrange flowers) if they came from other districts. They appreciated staying here because of the large garden which has an abundance of greenery which they were welcome to use for their demonstrations. I learnt a great deal from those skilled demonstrators and so I always had a large arrangement on my hall table and in the lounge, I even was able to do the flowers for my daughter's wedding. The demonstrators would keep their flowers in my garage overnight when necessary. Most flower arrangers are female but there are a few male ones too. One of those was a lively character and when he was here, he shared the breakfast table with a young family. The children had cereal and then wanted to get down from the table to play. I came through the swing door holding a full teapot and had to stop quickly as there he was, lying on the floor helping to amuse the three-year-olds with a colouring book and crayons. I was concerned that I might have spilt the hot tea over all of them! He loved children and played 'Peep Bo' with them, making them laugh. The parents were delighted as he kept the children entertained so that they could enjoy their breakfast in peace.

He was just delightful and even gave me some tips on how to preserve flowers. He came a couple of times and in his speech on the nights of the demonstrations on the stage in the town hall he said that he loved coming here and what a lovely place he was staying in. Very often these people would leave me any flowers left over and so they were very welcome guests indeed!

Lawnmower

Now this is a first which probably will never happen again (but you never know!).

I like to do the weeding and the annual planting in my flower beds and tubs, but I do have help with the heavy work in the garden like cutting hedges, moving heavy plants, digging, repairing the fences etc. My helper hurt his back and could not come for three weeks. It was growing season and the grass had been lawn sanded and so it was growing fast. By the end of four weeks, it was approaching eight inches high. As it was now going into high season, for tourist visitors I decided to get my new standby lawnmower out of the garage and tackle the job myself. I have an electric mower as I do not have the strength to pull start a petrol one. I had bought it for emergencies, and this was that emergency. I have three grassed areas in the front garden, and I struggled doing one as although the mower hovered it was still heavy. The next day I got the help of a kind neighbour who helped me raise the cutting blade because the grass was so long. Even with this it was still a hard slog. To make matters worse the weather was an unseasonal heat wave!

The day after that I started on the back garden and got

half of one area done. During one of my rests a couple arrived for B&B. I showed them into their room and took the usual fresh milk and biscuits through to them. After a while the wife came through and talked about the lovely garden and how she also loved gardening. She asked if I had help as the garden is quite a size. I said that yes, usually I did but that my gardener was suffering with his back right now, so I was doing it myself till he recovers. I mentioned the mowing and she saw the mower out back and said, "Oh, Ben will do that for you!" I didn't think she was serious as when they came in, he had said he was tired after a long drive and was going to nap before they went out to dinner.

A little while later the wife came to me and asked, "How do you start the mower?"

"You're not serious – it's very kind of you but really…?"

She interrupted and said that her husband Ben had obviously needed his nap and so she had decided she would do it. There was no need for her to do that, but I am constantly amazed at what people will do and say.

"Yes, I love gardening," she said, "and I've been sitting too long in the car, and I need the exercise."

"Well, if you'd really like to…" I said, and we headed out to the mower.

She marched over to the mower, picked up the cord and flipped it over her shoulder and after a quick easy lesson she started moving it over the lawn (albeit fairly slowly).

After a while she asked if she could have a glass of water. She had worked up quite a sweat.

"Of course, please sit down and would you like a drink of juice or a beer maybe?"

"No, no just water."

I brought the water and said for her to sit down and rest in the shade as it was so hot. We chatted for a bit then she stood up to go again.

"No really, you have done enough."

"Yes, yes I've started so I'll finish." She smiled quoting from the TV programme 'Mastermind'.

And she did, God bless her, and she even spied another area of grass unseen from the windows.

I knew that she wouldn't accept money, but I said to her to help herself to anything from the souvenir table in the lounge.

"No, not at all I enjoyed doing it," she insisted.

To have people like that arrive just when I needed them was an act from the angels indeed!

Thank you, angels!

The Wedding Anniversary

This is another one from the angels! A couple from Perthshire booked in for a three-night stay and while booking on the phone the husband told me that it was their thirty-fifth wedding anniversary – the coral anniversary. I said that was lovely and congratulations. From this conversation I could tell that he was a bit of a joker. He went on to tell me that his wife had told him that what she would like for her present was a piece of coral from the Caribbean.

"Well," he said, "that's maybe what you want honey but what you're getting is a fish supper from Ayrshire!"

Should be an interesting visit, and so it turned out to be…

As they had no car, I picked them up from the railway

station and we happily chatted immediately. As there was a church fete on that morning, I asked them if they would like to see it on the way up. They did, and enjoyed an hour and a half looking round then had a coffee and a scone and I bought some garden plants. They were delighted to be talking to the locals!

The husband walked with one crutch, and it transpired that he had had a couple of mini strokes but had recovered enough to walk again. He had been in a wheelchair for a year but was determined to get back to normal.

They were a very nice loving couple and very entertaining to listen to.

In the evening they wanted to sit out and enjoy the balmy evening air. It was still early in the year and my garden furniture was not yet out in the garden. I explained that my garden helper was off sick and that the table was still in the garage and needed re-assembling. I said I would bring out some chairs from the house for them.

"Have you a screwdriver?" he asked. "I'll do the table for you."

"Oh, thank you so much but there's really no need," I said. "I can bring out a small table from the conservatory for you."

"No," he said, "I like to feel useful."

So, after a lady cutting my grass, here was a guy assembling my table!

When he finished, I said, "That calls for a glass of wine. Would you like one?"

Luckily, I had a bottle in the fridge, and I joined them for a while. We had a good chat and they told me how he had had Polio when he was young then the stroke and how he had struggled to get back on his feet. His determination was inspiring, and it shows how much a strong will is so important in convalescence.

That night while thinking about them I decided to give them a gift for their anniversary the next day. I had two pieces of coral from the Caribbean. I was lucky enough to have been to several islands in the Caribbean some years before and had brought back two lovely coral souvenirs. I didn't need two pieces so I wrapped up one, put it in a fancy bag and put it on the breakfast table. I told them it was a genuine piece of coral from the Cayman Islands in the Caribbean. They were clearly delighted (a few tears) and hugs were exchanged.

That day they had the celebratory fish and chips for lunch and spent the afternoon on the beach as the weather was wonderful. That evening they came in with three bottles of wine for the fridge and asked for wine glasses.

They asked me to join them this time with their wine. I just had one glass but by the time dusk had fallen two of the bottles were empty!

Each evening they enjoyed having their wine on my patio surrounded by the pots of flowers. It was the time for the laburnum to be in bloom and they kept asking what it was called as they had not seen one before. It is a really lovely tree with long yellow flowers and is beautiful beside the purple rhododendrons. Almost everything in the garden was photographed (including me) and they were intrigued by the face, 'Mr Tree', on the oak tree at the entrance to my property. This is made of three stone pieces from Florida which are fashioned and painted into a face – eyes, nose and mouth. It is very common over in Florida but not as well known here. It is certainly something appreciated by young visitors and quite a talking point. For one little boy I tried a bit of ventriloquism. I asked him if he would like to speak to Mr Tree and when he said, "Hello, Mr Tree", I made the tree speak back to him asking him questions. The boy went round the back of the tree looking for the rest of Mr Tree. I told him that he was inside the tree. The boy went away looking back at the tree as he walked with his mother to their car.

The anniversary couple also loved the cooked breakfasts having worked their way through the choices with any combination of and the guy was funny. When he had finished each day, he said he was counting the hours before he had the next one!

People like these are the reason I love my job! With almost Caribbean weather while they were here, I think they had a very happy anniversary.

Talking of 'talking points', I have another one. On the wall just as you go into my lounge, I have many bank notes pinned up. This is now called 'The Money Wall'. I saw this in restaurants in the US and it gave me the idea. I had several different currencies from my travels and so I pinned them up for interest. People come into the lounge, stop when they see the notes, talk about them, and then study them to see if their country is represented. Over the years people have added to them and they would say, "Oh, you don't have one of ours," then would search in their pockets or wallets and pin them up. Some of the notes will be collector's pieces now as several countries being in the EU all have the Euro. I have two notes from Hungary denoting 500,000 and 100,000 lira. A tiny note from Beijing which looks like monopoly money and is probably worth about one penny! People don't believe that it is real, but it is. An Indian gentleman gave me some rupee notes and also some from Bangladesh saying that I would probably never get any of those as the people of Bangladesh are mostly too poor to travel. The notes are so dirty and old they are barely legible but still interesting. It all adds to the reality. It's amazing how different these notes can be. The latest in this large collection is an unusual one from Iceland. I had never had people from there before and so it very special to have their Krona. People love adding to the wall and some even have sent some over from home if they had not had any with them while they were here!

I have sixty-three countries so far – only one hundred and forty-three to go!

Near the money wall I set up a souvenir table shop for tourists because not having a tourist office in the town there was nowhere for them to find information or little gifts to take home. It started when someone asked me for postcards and so it began from there. I added to it following different requests. A memorable request was for a 'See you Jimmy' hat – this being a red tartan beret with orange fake hair attached to it. This was duly added. I found some with a button on them and when you pressed the button it played the sound of the bagpipes! This went down particularly well with Americans.

Chapter 11

Arrival Times

The time when people arrive at a B&B is one of the most difficult and frustrating things for the house owner. This is particularly so if there is no 'staff' on site at all times.

On the face of it, asking people what time they will arrive is a simple and straight forward way to know approximately when your doorbell will ring. Approximately is the relevant word but can mean 'All things to all men'.

A couple were due to arrive at Glasgow Airport at four p.m. It is a forty-five-minute drive from there to here and perhaps a thirty-five minute add on if they are hiring a car. At the time of the booking by phone I told the guest I was going out at six p.m. and wondered if they could come along as quickly as possible so that I would be there for them.

I had arranged with friends to meet up and have a meal then go to the local cinema. I would meet them there after seeing in the guests. Five p.m. came and went, six p.m. also, so I called their mobile number, but it was switched off. I kept in touch with my friends giving them updates as time went by. I looked up the flight on the internet and saw that it had arrived on time so where were they?

At seven p.m. they finally arrived full of exasperation about the unhelpfulness of the car hire people. (Not, you note, full of apologies for me!) Apparently at the car hire desk they were asked for £600 cash deposit (which of course they did not have – who carries that amount with them?) and credit cards were not acceptable. So, what were they to do? ATMs only give out £350/day. Eventually they went to a different car hire desk where they had no trouble at all AND it cost them £50 less for the hire!

Anyway, I said, "Here is your room, sorry I have to dash as I am so late now…"

"Oh," the woman said, "I didn't realise you were waiting in for us!"

Even if we had not had the conversation about me going out that night it would have been good to call and say 'Sorry, we're held up at the airport'. Or even to say, 'Keep the room for us we're still coming!'

They were going straight out too so having seen them away I dashed off, had the fastest bite to eat ever with my friends who had long since finished a full meal and rushed over to the cinema. At the desk we were told, "Sorry, too late. The house is full!"

All we could do was have a coffee then go home. I felt so bad for my friends missing the film. Had we known from the guests in time then my friends could have gone in and got the tickets and one for me then I could have joined them later.

Arrival Times – A Classic!

Most B&Bs have a network whereby if they are full then they will pass people over to each other.

This happened recently to me. I was expecting a father and his two sons to arrive around eleven a.m. from a B&B

which could not keep them for the third night they required. That morning I had planned to go to the local post office to collect a parcel which had been delivered to me the previous day when I was out. The post office collection office closes at noon and so I had thought I had plenty of time to be here for the guests then go to the post office for twelve. Eleven came and went as did twelve – wouldn't get the parcel now till tomorrow. At one fifteen p.m. I phoned the other B&B to ask when their guests had left and what their plans were. I was told that as far as she knew they had been coming straight over. However, they also were going to visit relatives at some point and so between us we decided that they would not now perhaps arrive till the evening. It was a pity they did not have a mobile phone.

That decided I went off to have a bath. My bedroom is not ensuite and so I take my bath or a shower at times when guests are not in to keep them free for the guests later. A daytime bath is a luxury usually taken occasionally after all guests have left and the rooms are turned around for the next visitors.

Yes, you've guessed it, the very second I had lowered myself into the bath, I thought I heard a car drive into the driveway! That bathroom is directly over the driveway. Oh no, surely not! Sure enough, I heard car doors shutting and footsteps coming to the front door. What to do? Go to the door in a towel? I think not! Do I get dressed and by the time I reached the door they would be gone? No, I decided to ignore them as, after all, they should have arrived over two hours ago and this is not a hotel! They could just come back. About five minutes later I froze as I heard a voice in the kitchen (which is underneath the bathroom) calling,

"Hellooo!" Help! I had locked the front door but obviously not the back door! Now, while I'm thinking what on earth to do, I couldn't believe it when I heard someone coming up the stairs! Then they came along the corridor towards the bathroom (which was luckily locked but I looked at the door anyway in consternation!). Whoever it was realised I was in the bathroom as I heard an "Oh" and they went back downstairs again and eventually drove off. Now I started to get angry and thought, *What kind of people go round the back of your house and enter and then go UPSTAIRS?*

When dressed I phoned the other B&B and she was horrified and we decided the guy was slightly strange (though harmless). This was an impression we'd both had from previous conversations with him.

Just after this phone call the doorbell went again. On opening I saw it was the guest with his two sons.

"Hello," I said, "come in. Were you here about fifteen minutes ago?"

"No," he said, "it wasn't us," and the way he said it as he looked at the floor made me think he was lying and didn't want to admit he had been in the house. Then I noticed his face was bright red spreading down to his neck and so I was convinced he was lying and thought, how can he lie like that in front of his children? I looked at him sceptically and raised one eyebrow, but he was adamant, so I just carried on with the welcome and showed them into their room.

In the middle of the afternoon, I suddenly remembered about the person who was staying for a few days for golf and had told me he would be back around one or two p.m. to shower then go for his round.

Oh no! It must have been him! He had the front door

key, but as I had locked the door before bathing, he couldn't get in as I had left my key in the door!

When he came back he said he had gone round the back, was reluctant to go into someone's house but needed his things, had gone through the kitchen then upstairs – quite legitimate as his room was upstairs!

SO, you should never jump to conclusions! The poor guy with the sons was telling the truth and his red face and neck were due to sun burn from golf the day before! Thankfully he didn't seem perturbed by my 'welcome' and was perfectly chatty for the rest of their stay.

Phew! What a day.

An Unhappy Lady

Yes, really, arrival times are hard to get right especially when you are on your own with no one to be there if you are out. For guests too, arrival times are inevitably an estimate, hence ETA in the travel industry. Guests can under or over-estimate their journey time and so can arrive hours before or after their stated time. Sometimes they will phone to tell you of a problem but sometimes they don't. I have often waited and waited for many people – some seem to think it's like going to a hotel where as long as they arrive that day the timing doesn't matter too much. They don't perhaps realise that B&Bs can be a private house where the host has a schedule. I always do my best to be there for when people are due to arrive. Occasionally things happen beyond my control (or the people are early!) and I come back to see guests waiting for me. Most people when this happens are sympathetic when they hear the reason and are not too much bothered.

One woman arriving with her mother was very bothered! I arrived just ten minutes after her expected time. I was hurrying to get back to get home in time but arrived to see a note stuck to the front door. It was angry writing (you can tell!) saying that they had arrived early and how dare I not be there (her words). If I couldn't be there when guests arrive, I shouldn't be doing B&B! They had waited till their expected time then left. No mention of whether they were coming back or not so I could not re let the room in case they did. The area was busy that night with several events on, so I wonder how long it took them to find somewhere.

Chapter 12

<u>Employing the Family</u>

When my daughter was about fifteen, I asked her if she would like to act as a waitress at the breakfast table (for a little pocket money of course!) and when she thought about any monetary tips she might get too, she agreed. One difficulty she had to really overcome was to get up in the morning early and, like most teenagers, this was not easy! It also involved me running up and down stairs now and again to see if she was up and giving the necessary prod! However, things went mostly smoothly but a couple of times things would go awry. The first problem was caused by an actor who was over here from America for a show in Glasgow. He stayed at the coast as he wanted to play golf in between times. Incidentally, he had a Filipino wife who was treated shamefully like she was a slave. She was a lovely little girl who hung on his every word (but almost as if she was afraid of him). He did not chat with her and only spoke with her when he was instructing her. While he was playing golf, I offered to take her around the town and show her the sights but she politely refused saying she would need to stay in the room in case her husband came back and needed her. I wonder how long she stayed with him. She probably was sending money back home to her mother and family so felt trapped. This man's name was Baurm and with his American drawling accent it sounded like Bum. Lorna said no way could she serve him breakfast as she couldn't stop giggling at the thought of serving a Mister Bum!

Another little faux pas was a morning where we had six people at the table and they all wanted different breakfasts. When all were served, I noticed I had one sausage left in the pan. I asked Lorna to go through and see if anyone was missing a sausage. Sure enough, she came back through and said that someone was. I put it on a saucer and gave it to her to take through to the table. She came back with a typical teenage act of her hand over her mouth, eyes huge, and laughing hard with embarrassment.

"What? What?" I said, smiling. I had assumed that she would put the saucer with the sausage on it beside the woman's plate. Instead of which she 'sheuched' the saucer with a flicking motion of the wrist to slide the sausage on to the waiting plate. As she did so she said, "Here's your sausage." The sausage flew off the saucer, missed the plate and bounced onto the table cover then on to the floor! At least the incident gave the breakfast party some entertainment, but poor Lorna was purple with embarrassment! The waitress employment did not last long as the early rising did not go down well, and the tips were not as lucrative as she had hoped! This incident was, forever more, known in the family as the "Here's your sausage."

Lorna's help was, however, a great help in the 'Panic of the tourist board inspection'.

The Tourist Board Inspection

After several years of reasonably trouble-free guest house running I decided to go for the grading and classification by the tourist board. Soon it was going to be compulsory to have a grading in order to be a member of the tourist board. The grading is dependent on the amenities and quality of fixtures and fittings.

The visit by the inspector is supposed to be incognito so that they get to know how it really is for the visitor and not just the best of everything for the inspection. This is a good theory but in practice you generally know who it is before they come. Not that you would ever acknowledge that at the time and indeed you would feign surprise when informed after breakfast that that is who they are! Guest houses are inspected annually and so when your turn is due from the previous year you are waiting for the phone call for a booking for a single person (usually female) and somehow, they just don't sound like a tourist – although you can't totally rely on that. As the inspectors come from Inverness, they usually visit all the B&Bs in each town one after the other. When the first one has the visit, the owners then call the other B&Bs to tell them 'The inspector's in town!'

In the first year of being visited, all summer long hosts are waiting for 'the call' and several false alarms ensue! Any single person booking in, whether male or female, they are all suspects. (Not every inspector is female!) Any single booking creates a mad dash to go round each room and make sure everything is as perfect as possible. If it turns out not to be the inspector, then there is a slight feeling of anti-climax in knowing you will have to go through it all again. When they have arrived and gone then you can relax and enjoy the rest of the season.

Grading starts on your response to the enquiry –

friendliness, helpfulness and ease of booking.

The criteria for grading at that time was – at least one chair for a single room, two chairs for the twin and double rooms, matching bedspreads (they were anyway), matching bedside lamps, good quality towels, curtains, carpets and all bedding, a good supply of tourist leaflets, and a bounteous hospitality tray. I was once pulled up for having 'naked' tea bags! I had a dish of sachets of coffee, de-caffeinated and regular, brown and white sugars, sweeteners, hot chocolate, fruit and spiced teas etc, but I was temporarily short of black tea sachets and had put in some tea bags from my own cupboard. How could I have forgotten that one?

One of my bedroom doors had no key for the lock. There was a bolt on the inside of the door but a lock with key is mandatory. After all, if the guest locked the door with the bolt and something happened to the guest then you couldn't get in to help. I thought I could easily get a key from the local locksmith. Well, of course, it was not that easy! No key for that kind of lock was available. His only suggestion was a key which would work from the outside only. I couldn't see how that would work but I had no time to have the whole lock replaced and so that would have to do in the meantime.

Having been warned by another B&B that the inspector was in the area I received a booking which fitted the bill. The inspector duly arrived and was shown into the room, given the friendly chat and asked for breakfast preferences. All seemed fine. After she went out again for a meal, I decided to make sure the key worked properly as I had not had time to try the lock with the door actually shut. I had just quickly tried it with the door open. I was surprised to see that she had not locked the door when she went out. I closed the door again and locked it.

OK good, it locked. It was then I found I couldn't unlock it! Can you imagine the panic? Of all people to be locked out! The only other way into the room was via the window either standing on a chair on the flower bed or a ladder! I had visions of pushing her in through the window and out again in the morning complete with luggage!

Eventually after much jiggling the door opened but I couldn't risk that happening to the inspector. I could see that the problem was the lock which was slightly out of alignment with the wall and the lock was slightly too high therefore the key was slightly hitting the metal instead of slotting inside. I called for daughter Lorna's help! We searched in the cupboard where the tools were kept and found no sign of any rasp to file down metal! Eventually in the garage we found an old pretty rusty rasp. Whew, that would have to do.

"Right, Lorne," (as we called her at home). I said, "You watch the front door (which is glass) for her coming back while I try to rasp away the metal." As I was desperately pushing the rasp backwards and forwards pieces of sawdust and metal were falling from the wall. I was making a real mess and Lorna started laughing. Soon I was laughing too, and hysteria set in. It is not unusual for us to giggle at quite inopportune moments. This, however, was not funny! She then brought out the vacuum cleaner and sucked up the droppings as I rasped while we both kept an eye on the front door.

At last, the key turned a little more easily and when the inspector returned, I just said casually, "Take care when using the lock as there is a knack to it!" She smiled and I went upstairs and looked back over the banisters to see how she managed but heh, it worked! Phew!

In the morning she was leaving and so she wouldn't need to lock the door. She didn't mention it, and everything worked out fine! The only thing she found to comment on in her inspection was that the milk jug did not match the breakfast crockery. I explained to her that I did indeed have a matching one and used it for a single person but that it was too small to hold enough milk for more than one person. In my mind a bigger glass one was universal and much more practical! She just said, "I see," and offered no more comment.

Last Inspection

My last inspection before leaving the tourist board was not without incident either.

The latest 'new idea' from above was that every room which was not en-suite should have bath robes available for those who emerge from a room to walk across to the bathroom or shower room to bathe or shower. Now, most people who go to a B&B either take their own or don't feel the need for one and I have never been asked for one (OR hand lotion or cotton buds which she was also suggesting!). I do have make up remover pads in little glass containers with lids. This was not commented on, just the 'missing' items.

Incognito stay-overs by the tourist board are only carried out by the inspectors every two or three years with the intervening years having prearranged visits.

This upcoming visit was a prearranged one. A friend, who runs a B&B in another part of town and I decided that we were not going to go to the expense of buying robes which no one would ask for and so we came up with a plan. We each had two bath robes of our own which had never been used. Our visits happened to be on the same day. I was to be visited first on the day and the day before my visit I went over to the other B&B and borrowed her two robes.

Apparently, all that was required was that there should be a notice in the rooms saying 'Bath robes available on request'. I put the notices in the rooms and the four bath robes put aside in case she asked for them. The inspector finished around noon and was very satisfied (no naked tea bags this time!) and I asked her nonchalantly what she did for lunch. "Well, I just usually have a banana and a cracker in the car."

I knew that she was having her lunch break before going round to the next one, so I said casually, "There is a really nice area down near the harbour where you can park and watch seals at play." This, I knew, was the furthest point from her next appointment and to give me time to take the robes round.

"Oh, that would be great," she said. "That sounds like an interesting place to go to so I will do that!"

I gave her directions and off she went. I called ahead to say I was coming and grabbed the bath robes and rushed out to the car and drove round to the next 'victim'.

"Thanks," she said. "How was it?"

"Fine," I said, "and she didn't even ask to see the robes or seem to see the notices in the rooms or mention anything about the new rules!"

I telephoned later that day and was informed that she wasn't asked for them either!

I had come across this before. On one visit I was asked

for the cereals to be decanted into Tupperware tubs with labels on instead of them being still in their boxes. I personally think it is better for the guests to see that you are actually using Kellogg's instead of the cheaper supermarket brands. Also, it is not unknown for hosts to fill their tubs with cheap versions and if they are just being topped up all the time then the pieces at the bottom could be old and soft.

For the next visit I still had the boxes and wondered what this different inspector would say. She did not mention it. Nor did she mention the cotton buds and hand lotion. You would think, and expect, that the inspector would have a note on your file about the last visit's findings! I suspect it is a case of whatever each individual inspector thinks and not what is laid down!

Panic Abroad

When I am at home to organise things and keep things running as smoothly as possible then usually all is well. The minute I go on holiday despite making copious plans beforehand, things very often happen the likes of which do not seem to happen when I'm here.

For example, my self-catering apartment was let to holiday makers. Guests were in before I left, and I had asked them to put the keys back through the letterbox on leaving. That was fine they did that. I had asked my cleaner to do the turnaround for the next guests who were due the following week and I had given her the dates and time of arrival. The cleaner had not been with me very long but had been efficient so far. I asked her to leave the key for the guests in the flower trough at the front door. The entrance is indoors, being an apartment, and they had instructions for the main building entrance.

On the day of arrival, I received an email from the guests saying there was no key. Oh no! I called the guests and apologised and suggested that they ring the next-door neighbour's door (on the same floor) as they hold a spare key. No reply – they were out. Oh no! I called the cleaner, but no reply and I left a message. The guests said they would go to the relatives, whom they were here to visit, and wait there till I found a key. I felt so helpless being so far away and not being able to contact anybody. I eventually called my 'Guru' Marion as she lives near the address of the cleaning company and, bless her heart, she went round to the address only to find that the company had moved some time ago and had not updated their website! Oh no! Next thing was that the guests emailed me again and said that if I did not come up with a key by six p.m. they would go to a hotel and charge me with the cost! You can imagine the upset I was feeling at not being able to sort this mess myself!

At about five thirty p.m., my neighbour at last answered my desperate phone calls. Hallelujah! She would give them the key.

I emailed the guests who then went round for the key. I relaxed for the first time that day.

Not for long!

I received an irate message from the guests saying that yes, they were in, but the place had not been cleaned! The beds were not done, and the bin had not been emptied and the oven was dirty. I was really upset and wondered could this get any worse? Apparently, as I learned later, the cleaner had been in that morning but didn't finish and took the key with her as she was coming back. She claimed that she did not know the guests were coming in that day. All I could do was to apologise to the guests again and say that she would come back in the morning and that I would refund half of their money.

In the end the guests really enjoyed their stay (after the cleaning!) and actually booked again for the next year. They appreciated the lengths I had gone to to solve the situation. Phew!

Other things I came back to over the years were not human related. I had planted forty tulip bulbs in the two flower beds edging the front path of the house. It was a particularly cold winter and the squirrels had been busy. I have a large oak tree at the entrance to the property and it is entertaining to watch them running up the tree, collecting an acorn and then running down and burying it in the garden. They seem to bury their winter store randomly and I would find little saplings all over the place throughout the year! That winter they must have not been able to find their hoard (or had eaten them all) and so had started on the tulip bulbs! They must have been able to smell them (or were watching when I was planting them!). When I returned, instead of seeing a path of colour, all I could see were the forty holes each with the brown skin of the bulb lining the hole!

Another year I came back to find twenty-five mole hills in the grass in the back garden. It took several years after that to rid the grass of mole activity having tried mole smokes, traps, and the services of a mole catcher.

One time it was Otto who alerted me to a squatter who had taken up residence. A couple of days after returning I was watching TV one evening. Out of the corner of my eye I saw

Otto staring fixedly at something under the radiator. He would then paw at it. I wondered if it was a mouse perhaps, so I went over to see and sure enough it looked like a mouse hiding there. I wondered how I was going to catch it without Otto getting it first. I wanted to put it out into the garden. The thing came out and I realised it wasn't a mouse at all it was a frog (or a toad)! Where on earth did that come from? All the doors and windows had been shut. Otto pawed it and it hopped round the lounge while I thought how to deal with it. Firstly, I picked up a magazine and got it onto it. While going to the door the frog hopped off. Hmmm, that worked well! Next, I found a large jar and put it over it, then slipped the magazine under it and managed to get the frog outside. I couldn't think where it had come from because I don't have a pond in the garden and the nearest one is further down and across the road in a neighbour's garden and it was in their back garden. Since then, I have had a newt seen in the garden so maybe they do go for walks around the neighbourhood.

Chapter 13

<u>Another Key Story</u>

It was the Tourist Board's fault really. Well, you have to blame somebody, don't you?

For the grading and classification from the national tourist board one of the criteria is again, as stated, to have all bedroom doors lockable with removable keys. Now, guests, as they do, sometimes go off with keys by mistake and sometimes they are sent back with apologies but sometimes they are not. It is expensive to have to keep replacing lost keys but maybe people think, 'Well, they probably have plenty of sets of keys.' Or again maybe they don't think like that at all and on finding the key they think, 'Oh well, I don't need that now' so they just throw it away!

This is what happened at The Cherries last summer. Not, you might think, a disastrous event but, as it turned out, it might have been.

Missing a key, I had two spare ones cut at the local locksmith.

Two couples booked in to attend a wedding. As they would be in late after the wedding, I arranged with them that I would leave the front door unlocked with the key inside and asked if they would lock it once they were in. This was the routine for anyone coming in late.

At two a.m., I awoke to the sound of someone leaning on the front doorbell. My first thought was that my son, Bob, and his friend, who was staying the night, had come in first and locked the guests out. Oh no! I scrambled up, threw on the nearest thing which came to hand – an old woolly jumper. I opened my bedroom door and saw the light was on in the upstairs guest bedroom. Oh, good, I thought. Bob has let them in, and I went back to bed. No sooner had my head touched the pillow when the bell sounded again! I crawled out again, pulled on the old woolly jumper again, opened my door and looked over the banisters.

"What's going on?" I mumbled woollily.

As I looked down, I saw one of the wives sitting on the hall chair and when she saw me, she was saying, "Shh… she's here!" The husband came in off the doorstep and they said in unison, "We can't get into our room!"

"What?" I said as I stumbled down the stairs in my bare feet. I tried their key and all the jiggling in the world wouldn't open the door. My mind started racing. This was one of the new keys I'd just had made. Oh no, I hadn't tested it! (Lesson to learn!)

"Don't worry," I said. "I have the master key – I'll get it for you." I came back with the master key and tried the door. It wouldn't budge! This is not happening, I thought, it's a nightmare, please let me wake up! By this time the upstairs couple had joined us, and everyone had a go at jiggling the door. The poor wife on the chair was obviously desperate to get to bed (or go to the loo!) and I was wishing I was anywhere else! The two husbands were busily deciding the best course of action with whisky breath thick in the air. We all must have looked a pretty sight – them in their finery, although the men's ties were hanging loose, and me in my nightdress, bare bunioned feet, no make-up on, and hair standing on end!

"Right," said one husband. "I am a joiner, I'll take off the frame of the door and cut the lock out for you – carefully, with no mess. You'd have to get a joiner tomorrow in any case."

With visions of him wrecking the door and the wall I declined his offer and suggested I give them a twin room for the rest of the night and deal with the problem in the morning (with them being sober!). I gave them coffee in the lounge, put on the TV for them, then flew upstairs and literally hurled my son and his friend's things out of their room into mine and did the fastest change of beds ever and looked out fresh towels for them. Reluctantly the guests accepted the rooms and I sat down at four a.m. and panic set in. What if I couldn't unlock the door in the morning? What if? What if?

I heard Bob and his friend arrive home not exactly sober themselves after their Saturday night out. They started to giggle when I relayed the happenings, and soon we were all rolling about and also saying, "Sh, Sh… they'll hear us!" No, it certainly was not funny, but we were becoming a bit hysterical! We gave up and went to bed. I tossed and turned and worried and was up an hour early to have another go at the door. As I was shaking the door, the other husband appeared and offered to shoulder the door as this would be the least damage if we just burst the lock. He was a large man and indeed this seemed the best option. I suggested I turn the key as he pushed. Just at the split second before he hit the door, it magically opened! He nearly fell into the room! To this day I don't know how it opened or why it stuck in the first place. I just thanked the angels and almost wept with relief. At least there was plenty for them to talk about at breakfast. There was a lot of laughter, and so I was happy that they were not too upset. When they were leaving, I did not ask them to sign the Visitors' Book! Incidentally, I then had the lock changed!

More Keys

Keys are difficult things. Yes, really. Because do you give people front door keys, or not? On the one hand, these people are strangers, and you don't normally give strangers keys to your own home. On the other hand, you can't stay in the house all the time and you don't want to have people waiting on the doorstep till you return (it has happened!). My rule of thumb is that I only give keys to people who are staying for several days and that gives me time to suss out their integrity.

Another difficulty with keys is – what do you do when guests are going to be late in and you want to go to bed early? If more than one group is going to be out late you can't ask them to lock the door when they come in as they may lock the others out. This can happen when 'one nighters' are in for a wedding etc and so you don't give them a key. My solution is to have the key in the front door on the inside and put the guests' names on a piece of paper attached to the door. Alongside the name is a box where they are asked to put a tick when they come in and a pen is left out for that purpose. The last ones to tick their box lock the door. That is a good theory, and it works well most of the time and guests are intrigued by this arrangement but of course sometimes people come in and forget the notice and so with a tick missing the door is left unlocked all night!

One night at one a.m. an incident occurred which hopefully will never be equalled!

Two Italian couples (not the same party coincidentally) were booked in for a wedding for three nights and so were awarded a front door key. One of the couples had very little English and we had several entertaining conversations due to their lack of English and my lack of Italian. There was lots of sign language. Both couples were going to be out late. Knowing that they both had keys and were happy and understood the key arrangement I went to bed content that they could all come in.

In the morning one of the couples came down for breakfast and I did my usual "Good morning, did you sleep well?" bit (complete with sign language of hands together at face to indicate sleep). Instead of yah, yah, very good, Lucio (I thought his name was pronounced 'Loocheeo' but he pronounced it as "Lootcho") and his wife Sophia gave me swaying hands and sad face. "Oh?" I said. "What happened?"

Sophia asked me, "Do you sleep this house?"

"Yes," I said wondering what was coming.

"Last night," Lucio says, "I key the door," (signing turning of the key), "You no in, I bell (miming pushing the doorbell) brrrrrrrrrrrrr, brrrrrrrrrrrrr, you no in, I see garage, I go garage, see lascala."

"Oh, no," I gasped, thinking of the old conservatory suite I have in the garage. "You slept in the garage?"

"No, no," he waved his hands again.

"In the car?" I ask horrified.

"No, no, I get lascala," he asks the other couple, who have now appeared, for the word (they are enjoying this hugely). They have a little more English than the others.

"Stairs," they say.

"Yes," Lucio continues, "I get stairs up wall, bathroom open..."

"Help," I thought with my hand to my mouth, this can't be happening! Lucio had taken the ladders from the garage and extended them up to the SECOND-FLOOR bathroom window which they had seen was open. He had extended the ladder and climbed up above the cars and stone driveway and climbed in the window. He had to climb over the wash basin to get in then had gone down the stairs, let his wife in, then taken the ladders down from the wall and put them back into the garage! All very noisy and I didn't hear a thing! It's a wonder the neighbours hadn't called the police. So much for neighbourhood watch! I was so shocked I just hugged them both and said, "I'm so sorry for you!" What had happened was that the other couple had thought that they were the last people in and so had locked the door and left their key in the lock. (Didn't they see the empty tick box? They all probably didn't completely understand the instructions!) When the key is in the door on the inside using a key on the outside will not work. They had actually heard the doorbell being rung and the commotion of the guy climbing in the window because their room was near the bathroom, and they had not long come in themselves. They said they had thought, "If the lady of the house won't answer the doorbell, then we can't!"

When you think about it, Lucio could easily have slipped sideways on the ladder and fallen on to the hard path and broken several bones or worse!

Amazingly, they were not too upset, and thought it would make a good story to take back home. They enjoyed a large breakfast with the other couple and even more amazingly they booked in for another two nights at the end of their holiday. On leaving, Lucio waved and called, "Margaret, next time, leave bathroom open!"

"I will, Lootcho, I will!"

Chapter 14

<u>Americans</u>

Let me say that I have nothing against Americans, in fact, some of the nicest people whom I have met are American, but they do provide the most incidents of all nationalities.

They have a reputation for being demanding probably because at home B&Bs are not as common as they are here, and they are used to having more items provided like in hotels than we tend to offer here in Britain. The weather also plays a part as normally it is much warmer in the US, particularly in the south, and so iced water is served automatically in restaurants even before asking and so, very often, they are surprised they have to ask for it here. Heaters in the bedroom are another frequent request as are face flannels too (face cloths to us!).

A strange phenomenon I have noticed from Americans is that very often they leave their bedroom doors open so their ablutions are visible to passers-by in the corridor or they will be seen chatting for hours oblivious to being overheard by the household. Is it sexist to say it is mainly men who do this? Well, they do! If their rooms are not en-suite they will leave their towels and wash bags in the bathrooms and shower rooms as if they are at home.

They like to chat at length to us which is usually

interesting but sometimes you are busy and constant interruptions can be frustrating as we are not in the business of being rude to people.

Loud they can be sometimes, but they mean well and are mostly genuine people. Strangely enough, much as they are used to almost universally giving tips for all services in the US, they are by far the worst of tippers over here and expect hotel services for the price of a B&B!

An example of this was a lone American golfer.

Many people come to our area to play the big courses such as Royal Troon, Turnberry, Dundonald, etc. and although some Americans have the best of golf equipment, they are not willing to pay high accommodation rates and so stay in B&Bs. Some time ago a retired American golfer booked into my cheapest single room at £17 (this was way back!). He booked through the tourist board and so I lost ten per cent of the rate because of the commission which made my total £15.30. As it happened, he got drenched playing Turnberry and asked if I had a drying room to dry his sweater and trousers and shoes.

"Yes," I said, "and, if necessary, I will put them in the dryer."

I carefully dried them overnight and gave them back to him all neatly folded and still warm from the dryer. His shoes had been put on top of the boiler carefully stuffed with newspaper to speed drying.

"Thank you," he said, putting them into his bag. He told me how nice it was staying here as he had stayed at Gleneagles Hotel (the 5-star hotel in Perthshire) the night before and paid £300 (!) for hotel and golf and had a dreadful night's sleep with people banging doors from one to three a.m. Mediocre breakfast and he thought the whole place could do with updating!

Next, he told me that the previous day he had met a couple in the car park of Royal Troon G.C. and had started talking to them. They had said they could get him on to the course. Casual chat? I don't think so!

"Well, I hope they got you a good discount for your round," I said knowing just how much it cost to play there.

"Oh, I just paid the slip – I don't worry about that!"

Then he paid my bill, "I have it right," he said giving me the £15 and three ten pence pieces! That, after me drying his clothes and shoes and not charging for the dryer! Unbelievable!

Another American golfer arrived wanting to play Royal Troon. His eyebrows raised when I told him the price of a round there but, nevertheless, off he went. When he came back, he was SO pleased with himself! He couldn't wait to tell me that he had deliberately waited around in the car park, and when a threesome arrived, he went to chat with them, and they suggested he join them to make a four as their guest which meant not only did he get a free round but a complimentary lunch too! What a brass neck! Related to the last guy, do you think?

More Golfers

Gregory Peck and Danny de Vito lookalikes!

Gregory, 6 foot 3", or 4, gorgeous looking with very smiley eyes and oozing charm which he knows how to use! Wee Danny had several carrier bags of sweets and chocolates in his room. Big bars of Bourneville chocolate, Mars bars and an unopened box of Roses chocolates (Maybe they're for me – it has been known!). Again, they had insisted on having my cheapest rooms but as usual their golf equipment was top quality, and they were playing Royal Troon, Turnberry, Gleneagles and St Andrews – the big four. They also ate at the expensive restaurants and hosted guests too. In their open luggage in their room I could see, while doing room service, wooden boxes of Havana cigars and large boxes of the most expensive golf balls. They had booked by phone from the US wanting a full week and would confirm later but didn't. The following weekend they then phoned to confirm but said it would not be the full week as they wanted to play Carnoustie on the East Coast as well. They would have four days for sure. I said that I had refused bookings for their dates and could they let me know ASAP how many days.

"Oh, we want to do right by you, Mrs M. We'll pay for the week anyway."

OK, fine. On leaving I re-iterated the discount I had given them for the weekly rate, but he said, "Oh, we'll go back to the daily rate cos we only had four nights." I therefore would lose out on that weekly booking despite the higher daily rate. Do I remind him of his statement to pay the week? I decided not to have a confrontation early morning (others around) and so I let it go but was annoyed. (I don't think I would do that now!)

However, they gave me the laugh of the week so they are forgiven slightly. On emerging from my room one morning ready to start breakfast I encountered Danny coming towards me in the corridor as he was heading for the shower obviously not expecting to see me so early. He was wearing only his boxers with one arm round his clothes and the other round his towel. Not having hands left to cover his top half he turned scarlet and started to bob up and down trying to cover himself. I pretended to ignore it and said cheerily, "Good morning," and went downstairs where I cracked up.

Gregory Peck heard him saying good morning and thought he was speaking to him and so he replied, and I heard Danny saying, "Just bumped into Mrs M – like this!"

I mean what was his problem? He did have his boxers on!

The next chuckle was after they left. I was doing out their room when I found out Gregory Peck's secret! In his waste bin were used lady's panty liners! Never thought of men using them! Maybe he had a drip problem! Just shows you – gorgeous hunks may not be all that they seem! (And the chocolates were not for me either!)

Chapter 15

<u>Bonuses</u>

This is a most unexpected and wonderful part of doing B&B. It is never expected, but it is a lovely surprise when it happens. It can be many different ways in which people express their pleasure at the service they receive.

One man phoned up after his stay to ask where I got the blackcurrant jam, he had been scoffing for the last two days! I explained that it was home made so then he asked me for the recipe!

It's the little things like that that just make your day!

I've been amazed at how many people bring gifts from home even before they have met me. One woman brought me a ceramic thimble from Austria. I don't collect them like some people do but it could start me. Another gave me a glass dish with fish round the edge from New Mexico and another gave me a couple of embroidered napkins which she had made in Belgium.

Three golfers from Germany so appreciated their stay and the simple things like allowing them to sit in the conservatory to smoke or have a glass of wine. When I supplied them with wine glasses, they wanted me to share the moment with them. I declined but it was a nice gesture.

The night before they left, they said they had something

for me. Would it be some German wine perhaps? No, they had bought me a really huge bouquet of flowers tied with lots of bows and ribbons! I gasped and did the double 'mwah, mwah' kiss on the cheek to each of them. I was so delighted.

Two young guys stayed for only one night. They had no car so used a taxi at night and said they would be late back. I thought they might possibly return the worse for wear and noisy but they returned by eleven p.m. quietly and rose on time for breakfast. Not only that, one of them bought from the souvenir table gifts for his children and his wife.

I have been given many gifts over the years – flowers, chocolates, thimbles from different countries, ornaments, money tips and even jewellery. One lady, also German coincidentally, stayed for a few days and her hobby was crocheting. When she left, she presented me with a set of circular potholder mats which I use to this day. I also have a glass kiwi from New Zealand, a little glass house ornament from Switzerland and a set of three mock ivory Buddhas depicting 'See no Evil, Speak no Evil, Hear no Evil'.

I had a couple who stayed here several times over the years and I always looked forward to their visit. The wife suffered from MS and one of her legs had lost muscle power. Although a very sad situation they did not let it get them down or stop their travelling. Her husband always walked behind her and kicked her left booted foot forward for her. It was comical to watch. As I have two steps down into my lounge/dining room I set up a table before the steps so that she would not have to go down them. On leaving one year they presented me with a hanging ceramic plant holder which, to this day, hangs in the corner of the lounge. Another year I had been telling them about my daughter's sports day at school. The new ruling for that year was that the winners of the races would not get any prizes because the losers would feel bad! I thought this ridiculous as children need to learn and have incentives to succeed in life. The couple obviously thought so too as they came back that night with a lovely china bowl in the shape of a swan and it had little plants in it with a card saying, 'For Lorna, winner of the egg and spoon race'. How nice was that?

Some people even offer to help me with the dishes or do my ironing! I do not take them up on their kind offer but it is always lovely to hear. Occasionally, people will invite me to join them for dinner in the town. Especially if they are ladies on their own and I have accepted on occasion and learned their life stories.

There was a woman who brought her elderly mother with her from Holland. Mother was very frail but wanted to come for a last visit to the place where she grew up. She was extremely anxious to come although her daughter knew she was not really able to cope with the trip. She suffered from Alzheimer's and talked of coming over constantly to the point where her daughter could not bear it any longer so decided to bring her. Mother walked with the help of a Zimmer frame and not knowing the circumstances I had booked them into the twin room which is upstairs. The daughter had not enquired about a downstairs room and that one was now booked and so I could not unfortunately give it to them. When they arrived, I was concerned about this and tried to find them a downstairs room elsewhere but there are not many B&Bs here with downstairs rooms and those which do were sadly all full. With difficulty, we managed to get her upstairs and after the journey she needed a nap.

When mother was asleep the daughter came downstairs

and was obviously very distressed and in need of a break all be it short lived. It was a beautiful warm afternoon and so I put a couple of chairs in the garden and sat with her for a while as she really needed to talk over her problems. As it was that time of day, I gave us both a gin and tonic and listened to her very hard life with her mum. The next day they both took a nap in the afternoon. When the daughter awoke, she saw that mother had 'escaped'. Apparently, she was prone to doing that now and again. Daughter panicked as she knew that mother didn't know where she was and could be anywhere. She was also amazed that mother had managed to go down the stairs by herself and lifted the Zimmer frame down the two steps at the front door.

"Don't worry," I said. "She has her walker with her so she can't have gone far and will be easily seen." The worry was that she might have reached the main road which had heavy traffic.

The daughter and I split up and went in different directions keeping in touch by phone and we found her quite quickly. We managed to get her back upstairs, but she was very agitated and shouting loudly and could not be consoled. The daughter agreed to me phoning the doctor who came out fairly quickly and gave her an injection and talked her back into calmness. I was very thankful for the visit and there was no charge for a home visit even for a foreign national. The daughter couldn't believe the free service. Once home I was sent a hand carved set of tulip book ends as a thank you for looking after them. Mother had made them in the care home where she spent her last days. All these items given to me are perks of the job and which I would never have expected. It really makes you feel that all the work involved is worthwhile and it is lovely to be appreciated.

Chapter 16

There's Always Some!

Not all guests are ideal guests. I would say that ninety-eight per cent are absolutely great and indeed I have become really good friends with several. That's the interesting thing about doing B&B you just don't know who or what is going to come in next! The thing is, you just don't know, and you have to think on your feet at all times. I like to think that it keeps your brain active!

I had an unusual booking which I thought at first would be wonderful. It was a booking for six people for six nights. Most people who book that length of time normally choose to have self-catering. Perhaps there were none available. I know mine was booked. The majority of B&B bookings are for short stays of one, two or three nights for events like weddings, funerals, parties, visiting relatives or people touring Scotland usually going up the West Coast and down the East usually ending at Edinburgh. For some strange reason I have never heard of anyone going up the East coast and down the West! I was so pleased to have this one – no bed changing for nearly a week – that is a real bonus! They were two women and four children, all girls. Still sounds good. However, assume nothing – ever!

On arrival, the children, all around seven years of age,

rushed in, past me, and two of them rushed straight up the stairs. The mums were still unloading the cars.

"Just a minute, girls," I called, "you don't know where to go, come down just now till we get organised."

The mums were not in yet and so I showed the girls into the downstairs bedroom. This started off screams of "That's my bed."

"No, that's mine," as they leapt on the beds and started bouncing up and down.

Then they rushed off upstairs again shouting, "Where's the other beds?"

"Come down, please," I tried again. As the mums were still not finished unloading the car, I decided to show the children, the upstairs rooms (to prevent them from going into ours!) and again there were yells of "That's my bed!"

"No, it's mine!"

While the mums were depositing the luggage the littlest girl with glasses ran around shouting, "Where's the kitchen, I'm hungry!" I patiently explained that they only ate breakfast here and that the kitchen was my room only. The mothers seemed to be too busy chatting and organising their luggage to bother what the girls were doing or where.

Thankfully, they went off to gran's house to eat. On their return I heard them not settling and as it was rather late, I went to investigate in case they needed help. They could not get the television to work. It was fine before they arrived as I had checked it. They admitted that they had tried different things and had obviously detuned it completely. I could not fathom out what was wrong so said I would have to look at it in the morning. Oh dear, five more nights of this? Help! That night I had nightmares about the children coming into the kitchen and getting burned trying to reach the bacon then having to be carried out in an ambulance!

The previous night I had asked them, as I always do, what they would like for breakfast and what time would they like it?

"Eight a.m. would be good."

That was fine and I was up at seven. By nine a.m. they were not even up! Five minutes past ten they appeared and at least were apologetic and asked for a wake-up call for the next mornings. I explained that a cooked breakfast was no longer available now that it was so late, and I had to go out, but I could give them cereal and toast. This was accepted gratefully.

With six people you always hope that not all of them will want a cooked breakfast or if they do then you'd like them ideally to have all the same choices. The next morning this time six out of six of them did want a cooked breakfast and not only that but all wanted different things! Scrambled eggs, fried egg and bacon, sausage, no sausage, no egg, bacon, kipper etc.

"Tea? Coffee?"

"Yes please, one of each, and hot chocolate for the children."

Well, it's my own fault I did ask!

Looking ahead I had thought to prevent spillage of orange juice for which young children are famous. Normally I put the juice on the sideboard beside the cereals for self-service. This, however, means the carrying of the juice to the table and one of them would be sure to spill it and so for them I placed the glasses on their places on the table. Great idea – until one barging child climbed on to her chair and nudged the table hard and spilled ALL of them!

Once the juice had been cleared up the meal went smoothly after that but of course by that time the children had spied the swing in the garden.

"Can we, can we?"

"Yes," I said (please do!).

Unfortunately, this resulted in them running in and out via the patio door of the dining room and thus depositing varying degrees of mud on the carpet! Twenty minutes later while I am in the kitchen clearing up, one mother comes in saying, "Sorry, Mrs M, but Karen has picked some flowers – but I've told her not to!"

"Thank you," I said with gritted teeth, "please make sure they don't."

Sometimes, doing B&B could create large dentist bills...

After they had gone out at almost midday, I examined the TV. The power was on but no sound or picture. What could they have done? I looked at the back of the set and discovered a very small red knob down in the corner. To press this, they must have turned the set round to find it, but they must have as after I pressed it the service returned. I had to reprogram all the channels but had at least saved a repair bill. At the end of their stay, I was not quite so keen to have large bookings of families!

Talking of young children coming into the kitchen, I did have one who did just that. She was about three to four years old. There is a swing door between the dining room and the kitchen, and she pushed it and came through.

"I want a bit of paper to draw on," she demanded. (What happened to 'I want never gets?') To have her leave quickly I gave her some paper. Two minutes later she was back. "I need a pencil!"

"What's the magic word?" I said testily.

"Please."

Another couple of minutes it was.

"I want a pen."

This was too much. I grabbed a pen and took her by the hand and took her back to her mother and said, "Sorry but could you keep Julie in here please because there are a lot of hot things in the kitchen and I don't want her getting burnt."

"Sorry," said the mother and kept her at the table. What was she thinking letting her daughter do that? Probably wasn't thinking at all! OR maybe she was the one who told her to 'Go and ask Mrs M for a pencil!'

Now if this other tale had happened early on, I think I would not have lasted long in this business!

I had a group come for two nights – two mothers and two children.

The first night I was wakened at about two or three in the morning with the sense that something was wrong. I lay for a little while listening to the sound of voices trying to hear what was going on. I decided there was a problem, so I flung on my robe and with great trepidation went along the corridor. I knocked on the door and when they opened it, I was aware of a horrible smell of vomit!

Oh no! One of the children, who was about eight or nine years old, had been sick all over the bed and the carpet! The mother was trying to mop it up with my best towels!

"Oh dear," I said, "let me do that." I asked if she could take her son through to the other room and I would clean up.

If there's one thing I hate, it's vomit. I almost prefer diarrhoea to vomit! I removed the towels and all the bedding and then scrubbed the carpet as best I could and remade the entire bed. I also brought them a plastic bucket in case of any more.

It was a while before I could go back to sleep.

In the morning there were abject apologies and they also informed me that he had indeed done it again. Thank goodness for the bucket!

Chapter 17

<u>Damages</u>

I have been very fortunate or lucky to have had very few thefts or damages. The only thefts I can recall were the loss of two towels which would not be the end of the world, but they were brand new and part of a set and I would not have minded so much if they had been older ones. To make matters worse the perpetrators were relatives of neighbours. They were young lads and so I assumed they had put them in their bags by mistake. I called them up and asked if this is what had had happened and was careful not to accuse them of anything. One asked the other and neither seemed to know anything about it but would ask their friends if they had come across them. Needless to say, no one did and so I was minus two towels. Because they were part of matching sets it meant that the other towels could not be used either as I could no longer buy any matching ones.

The other 'theft' was an alarm clock and room key. A family with two young children had stayed and after they had left, I did the usual clean. Having changed the beds and checked everything I saw there was no bedside table alarm clock. On phoning them I was told that yes, they had found the alarm clock. They had also found the room key (which I had not at that time noticed). The story was that the three-year-old had a habit of putting lots of things into her mother's handbag and this was where the clock and key were. Wouldn't you know if a clock and large key were in your handbag? Anyway, children are like that, and I did get them back. Talking of keys, I have lost several room keys over the years and only sometimes do people post them back. Generally, people will put the key in their pocket or handbag or sometimes attach them to their car keys. It is easy to forget about them. Because of this I had the bright idea of getting a large key fob, big enough that it would be easily found or seen. However, that didn't work either, as it was then too big for people to post back easily and so they didn't!

More

A party of Americans booked in having arrived into Edinburgh from Arizona. They seemed friendly and chatty. They requested breakfast at eight a.m. and as the other party I had in were also Americans who had asked for eight a.m. I agreed. At the breakfast table one of the women's faces told me she was not happy, and I guessed it was because she didn't like sharing a table with strangers. As they were booked in for three nights, I suggested that they split the breakfast times to give each other more space. I do my best to keep my guests happy! The woman said nothing, and I thought that maybe she was just a miserable woman!

After breakfast, her party came in and said they were leaving – change of plans. Now the weather was cold for June, and I had put the heating on again since I had guests. I asked if it was the weather or if they were cold and she said she was cold as they were from Arizona where eighty-five degrees is mild! They paid for one night and as they had been booked in by the tourist board it came to an odd amount because of the board's ten per cent commission. They waited for their change which included 20p. When they had left, I discovered the real reason why they had left. They had broken the towel rail off the wall and not confessed. And they had the cheek to take their 20p! Nor did they pay extra for leaving early. I did not say they should pay one of the night's cancellation fee, as I was sure they would refuse and I just wanted rid of them. Now, they were not young – well into middle age. You can understand young ones running away in embarrassment, but they were old enough to know better.

Toilet Seat

Damages tend to occur when people have had a few too many drinks and so become careless. Other causes can be young children, dogs or people just not being familiar with their surroundings. Six youngish Swedes booked in for a golfing weekend. They stayed for three nights. It was a wet weekend in September after a warm and sunny summer and they came in at night with very wet sweaters, gloves, shoes and club head covers. I offered to dry them for them in the tumble dryer. During the evening they were well into their single malts (that always makes me nervous). The next morning while doing room service I noticed that the toilet seat in the ensuite was cracked right through. What should I do? Do I mention it? Ignore it? Replace it and say nothing? Ask them to pay for it? I hate this!

I decided to give them the impression I expected them to pay and see what happened. If they did, well and good, if not

– well I tried.

In the morning two of them arrived first to the dining table and I asked, "I have to ask, guys, what happened to the toilet seat?" One, who unfortunately was the least smiley one of the group, said that he had not noticed and anyway had only used it once! (And this was relevant, why?) The other one said he had noticed it and that it was cracked through. They said they were sorry (but least smiley was obviously not).

I went to the plumber's merchant and purchased a new one. It is a very fiddly and awkward thing to fit a toilet seat! I left the bill on the bed…

The next morning the six of them came in together (frightened to come in alone?) and 'least smiley' had the bill in his hand. When it came for him to order his food he said, "We found this in the room."

"Yes," I said, and went on to the next one. He didn't pursue it.

While clearing their plates I asked if they would like to try the Scottish kippers tomorrow.

Amazingly they all said yes – except 'non smiley'!

"No," he said without a smile. I think he wasn't going to have ANYTHING I suggested!

"You're scrambled egg and bacon?"

"Probably," he snapped.

In the next two days the subject was not referred to again. The chat was all nice and normal except for non-smiley. I decided to ignore him especially as they would probably not be back anyway. As he was rather an obese guy, he was the most likely candidate for breaking the seat. Maybe he just felt guilty!

On the morning of leaving, they all paid singly – and shared the price of the toilet seat!

Result!

Hidden Damage

As well as the B&B I also have one self-catering apartment which is let out mainly to holiday makers. Because of this it is generally used during the summer months.

A couple from Denmark wanted the apartment for ten days in February. This was very welcome this being the low season. They had sailed across the North Sea to have their boat repaired in Troon which is not far from here. There is an excellent and well-known shipyard in Troon and as well as the car ferries for the islands, many ships from many places get repaired there. This couple were not the owners of the boat but had been commissioned to take the trip across and oversee the works for the repair. While the boat was in dock it could not be slept in and so they rented my apartment for the ten days. While doing 'the chat' I discovered that they owned a number of apartments which they rented out themselves and so they were familiar with rental procedures. We had a good chat, and they were very happy with the place, and they gave me a £100 deposit to be returned at the end of their stay assuming no loss or damage.

At the end of the ten days, I went to the apartment to inspect it and return their deposit. All very friendly and all seemed well, and I gave them their deposit back.

On cleaning the apartment later that day I was stripping the bed when I thought it seemed slightly damp and so I examined the mattress. I lifted it up and was horrified to find the underside absolutely soaking and the pervading scent told me the reason. They had very obviously turned the mattress over to hide it and in doing so had soaked the base also! I was quite dismayed and disgusted and really angry. To chat away and pretend that nothing had happened was just unforgiveable. I knew that they were not leaving town that day and that they were staying on board the vessel which although was not yet finished was able to be lived in. It was too late to go that day and so I decided to wait till the next day to give me time to decide what I was going to do and say. The following day (still mad), I went to the chandler's office to ask which boat was theirs. On the way there I had admired a huge motor yacht moored in the largest berth in the marina. It had caused quite a stir in the town as not many of that size have ever been seen in Troon! We're talking Oligarch type wealth here! Monaco eat your heart out!

Yes, it turned out to be the Danish 'boat'! Wow! This was not a boat; this was a SUPER YACHT!

I was given the security code for the marina gates and I approached the ship. I took in the electric dark glass patio doors of the rear deck which had a wonderful polished wood flooring and fitted seating in front of which (I saw later) were three inlaid wooden tables for chess on one, back gammon on another and a covered roulette table on the third. All the fittings were in gold and the shine from them was wonderful.

I saw no sign of life on board and as I hadn't seen their car in the car park, I realised that no one was on board and so I had to return the next day.

On arriving the following day, I saw that their car was there and so I parked my car and went over to the electric gates and hit the buttons of the security gates and entered again. As I approached the ship, I saw moving shadows inside, so I knew they were there. At this point I became very nervous as I was there alone and what if, once I was aboard, they kidnapped me, set off and dumped me at sea? Don't be ridiculous! What if they denied it? What if they refuse to give me back the damage deposit?

I had come this far and so had to go through with it. I cupped my hands to my mouth, took a deep breath and shouted, "Helloooo, Hellooo." I saw the figures give a quick start and I could just imagine them saying, 'Oh no, it's her!' then trying to decide whether to hide or not!

After a minute or two the guy came out on to the rear deck and when he saw me, he really gave a good impression of bluffing it out.

"Hello, Mrs M," he shouted waving cheerily!

"Permission to come aboard," I shouted.

"Of course, I'll help you across."

There was a movable set of steps on the quay side and when I climbed up there was a gap across the water to the deck. He took my hand and helped me on board. I didn't know what I was going to do if they did deny it, but I carried on anyway.

"I think you know why I'm here, Mr B."

"Oh, why?" he bluffed.

"The bed," I said.

"Oh," he said looking down at the deck. After a moment he sighed and said, "Yes, I admit it, it was my girlfriend. She drank too much the last night and had an accident in the bed." Then he shouted for her to join us. She came out and he told her why I was there, and she then looked very sheepish indeed and stood beside him. I told them that as renters themselves they would know how I felt and that I had given them their deposit back in good faith. They should have had the decency to return the deposit. Did they really think that it wouldn't be noticed? What if I had not discovered it and another guest had got into the bed? That didn't bear thinking about, did it? I then requested the deposit. They were both looking down at the floor and shuffling in embarrassment and looked so like naughty school children caught in the act that it was very difficult not to laugh. He told her to go in and get the deposit in cash. That was so that I didn't think their cheque might bounce. After profuse apologies he helped me back on to the quay side and I went away in great relief and had a good chuckle in the car. I would have loved to have seen over the ship but sadly that would not have been appropriate!

Chapter 18

<u>Open Offences</u>

This town and area is world famous for golf with the first ever British Open Golf Championship (now renamed just The Open) having been played at Prestwick in 1860. It was played there until 1925. The first Open in Troon was in 1923 and it returns there every seven to nine years.

The Open Seniors Championship is also played there in between times. The new course at Dundonald (not far away from here) is championship standard and is on the list to hold the Scottish Open which is held the week before the Open in July. It is also being touted as an Open venue in the not-too-distant future.

It used to be that for the period of The Open, and a few days before, accommodation providers had the opportunity to charge serious money for renting out their property to players, course officials, TV, Press and various celebrities. People, especially those who lived near the course, even rented out their driveways by the day as parking by the course is very limited. Nowadays, sadly for the residents, accommodation is now provided in local fields in the form of company provided tents, pods, and mobile homes thus much reducing the required housing lets. Fields are also now let for parking. Obviously, this is wonderful for the farmers who own the fields, and the shuttle bus companies who ferry the crowds to the course.

For The Seniors Open the amount people will pay for accommodation is much less than for The Open as the big players are no longer eligible to play and the numbers of players is less. Also, the prize money is less than for the more prestigious event. A number of the players are still well known but do not provide the same high interest as the current younger top professional people.

We were offering our house for rent but were not getting many enquiries and as time went by it looked like we may not get it let especially not being situated immediately by the course.

I received a call from someone who said he was a player and was looking for a place to rent for himself and his family. I decided to lower my expectations and offered a price lower than I wanted as I had never heard of this guy so thought he must be an outsider in the field. He agreed the price immediately and booked in for ten days. Great, it was not a big price but more than the normal rates. I decided to Google him and find out more about him and to my horror I found out that he was quite famous after all and a millionaire to boot! No wonder he accepted my price! I was annoyed with myself for not knowing his name, but at least I had it let.

For the period of the let I had booked a holiday to The Orkney Isles with Lorna and my cousin and his partner. When the family arrived, we stayed on with them long enough to show them around and had left written instructions on how to work everything e.g., the hob, oven, washing machine, dryer, dishwasher, TV, and hot water etc. They were supposed to pay a damage deposit on arrival (they were American and so it was in cash), but I forgot to ask for it in the excitement of settling them in and us leaving for Orkney.

Apparently, the wife had it in her hand and was going to hand it over, but Lorna heard the husband say, "Just leave it now," and so she didn't. The player was obviously the boss of the family and strutted about as if he owned the place and was very brusque and was the big 'I am'.

They seemed pleased and appreciative of everything and so we set off happily looking forward to the break having never been to the Orkney Isles and it was a while since we'd seen my cousin.

We had a wonderful week in Orkney with its amazing history (and amazing weather when we were there!). We visited Skara Brae, the Neolithic village ruins some of which had been discovered after a massive storm in 1850 when the severe winds blew off several tons of sand and soil to reveal the previously unseen and unknown site. It is now a World Heritage site and excavations are still ongoing.

Another fascinating visit was to The Italian Chapel which consists of two Nissan huts transformed into a highly ornate chapel by Italian prisoners of war who were captured in North Africa and transported to the island of Lamb Holm in Orkney. The prisoners were allowed to work with scrap metal and wood from a locally wrecked ship and they had fashioned these pieces into beautiful artwork and useful items. The huts were coated in cement to preserve it from the weather and pillars, Gothic pinnacles, an archway and a bell tower were constructed. The inside was lined then painted to depict brick walls, carved stone and vaulted ceilings. The prisoners also made friends with the locals who played sports and games with them.

We visited the Sheila Fleet shop and her jewellery workshop and also viewed the work of a tapestry designer and her workshop where I bought a print of a thirty-foot tapestry which was sent to Australia after three years in the making. This print (not thirty foot long!) now hangs in my dining room. We also visited the stunning St Magnus Cathedral in Kirkwall, the capital of Orkney. Rock climbing (The Old Man of Hoy rock is famous) and hiking are favourite sports and the freshest of sea food dining is a huge pleasure.

There are many separate islands of the Orkney Isles and from the one we stayed at to the mainland of Orkney we had to drive across the Churchill Barriers. These were built during World War Two by the islanders helped by the Italian prisoners in 1940. These Barriers were built to join up the islands to keep out the German U boats after one had slipped through and torpedoed one of our submarines – The Royal Oak, killing eight hundred and thirty-five of the crew. This is now a poignant diving site. The history in Orkney is immense and the islands can bear several return visits.

When we returned, home the family were still in the house, but were almost ready to leave. I asked them if they had had a good week and the player said they did but he had to apologise for an accident that they had had. He then informed us that they had broken one of the bedside lights in their room. He handed me six golf balls on which he had scribbled his autograph – totally illegibly. He said I could sell them from the souvenir table which I have in my lounge to pay for them! I did not think to tell him that he could use some of the unpaid deposit to pay for it. I did not know at that time of the other damage they had done and not told me about.

Actually, as it turned out, he would be very insulted to hear that no one wanted the balls, and I couldn't even give them away!

He was also very keen to tell us that he had got a hole in one during the championship and one of the sponsors for that hole had presented him with *one hundred and twenty-three* bottles of wine. He had been given one bottle for every yard at that hole! Had he left us one? What do you think? He probably had had them all shipped home.

To think that I had left them a bottle of my favourite wine as a welcome gift! Maybe they thought that the bottles in the wine rack were left for them too as the bin outside was full of their empties. I should have, of course, packed them away.

I found a vase of flowers in the kitchen and thought, oh well, that was nice, but I soon realised, they were old flowers ready for the bin. Oh well...

What I found after they had left was worse than the broken lamp. I discovered it in their bedroom although it was not immediately noticeable. I was cleaning and changing the room when my eye caught the fixing of the decorative canopy over the head of the bed. The large silver knob was squint! I went over to it and discovered that it had been torn out of the wall and they had obviously tried to repair it with putty then pretend that it didn't happen! I found the putty container in the bin! It was not the correct material for doing this and so the whole unit plus the putty came out leaving a large hole in the wall! I was furious at their duplicity and really regretted not asking for their damage deposit. I wonder what they had been doing to cause that to happen. Better not to think about it!

Chapter 19

The French Girls From Hell!

This is another tale from the apartment and one which could make me wary of letting ever again!

A French girl called to say she and her friend were in town and could they come along and view the apartment for rent? I agreed, saying 'certainly' as the apartment was available at the time, and, because they had no car, I offered to meet them at the railway station and pick them up with their rucksacks and one bag each. Since they were not familiar with the town, I gave them a quick tour showing them the famous golf course, the swimming pool, the beaches and where the supermarkets were. They told me they were not here on holiday but were researching how children's homes were run in Glasgow. This was for their parents who wanted to open a home in Paris. (Why then were they staying here, twenty-seven miles away and more importantly why not be staying in Glasgow, especially as they were not here on holiday?) I thought it was too early in the proceedings to ask the question.

Once at the apartment the first sign of their strangeness was that while being shown one of the bedrooms one of them asked if they could unplug the pay phone as she didn't like an electrical field near her whilst sleeping.

"Well," I said, "you have the overhead recessed lights and table lamp anyway so I don't really think there would be a problem but there is a long flex on it so you could put it at the other end of the room or even put it in a drawer of the chest." It could not be unplugged as it was wired into the wall. I wondered whether they wanted to run off with the phone + money but there wouldn't be much in it. We moved on from there and I forgot about it as you get used to people saying unexpected things.

Having approved the apartment, the girls said they would move in the next day. Fine, that was agreed.

Next day I collected them again from the station and took them across. They couldn't pay the full rent for two weeks because according to them they could only get money from the 'hole in the wall' once a week. I was not sure whether to believe them or not as we can get money every day at home or abroad. Reluctantly I agreed to one week in advance and they paid a deposit. As it was a Sunday, the balance for the week had to be paid the next day when the banks opened. (Didn't they have bank cards?) They signed the rental form.

The apartment needed a little decorating after a busy season and I had asked my decorator to give me prices. He could come over on the Tuesday and so I phoned the girls to say would they mind if he came in with me to measure up and I could collect their balance of rent at the same time. They agreed, all be it reluctantly.

On the Tuesday I had developed a raging headache which turned out later to be the start of a nasty flu and so when I went to the apartment, I was under stress to begin with. Wearing a mask, I met the decorator outside and we went up to the apartment. I was totally unprepared for what we would see. One of the girls was in the kitchen preparing a meal and the other was on the phone.

I said to the decorator, "We'll start in the lounge," and led him through.

While he was measuring up, I noticed that the kitchen table and two of the chairs had been moved into the lounge at the window. Well, that has been done before as the view from there is wonderful and sometimes people like to sit there as they eat. That was fine but then I saw that one of the twin beds had been dismantled and was stacked along the wall behind the settee. Why? Wait a minute – there's a blanket over the TV! What?

I became aware that the decorator was speaking to me.

"I'm sorry," I said. "I'm having difficulty in concentrating on what you're saying as I'm just noticing more and more unusual things here."

The blanket over the TV was not even a spare one taken out from the wardrobe in the main bedroom, but one taken off the bed! Hang on, the books have disappeared from the bookshelves! Even the children's books and all the ornaments have gone! Hey! The large picture has gone from over the fireplace! There had been a large four-foot-wide picture on the wall and now only the nail was left! Even the calendar had disappeared! The decorator was obviously wondering what was going on too. We moved on to the small bedroom—

"What the...?"

Not only had the one bed been moved into the lounge but the other bed had been moved to a different wall and the headboard had been removed! The dressing table had been moved to behind the door and a different chair was there. The chest of drawers had been brought in from the large bedroom and was sitting across the corner of the room. Again, the pictures had gone leaving only the nails. The long mirror was gone from the wall with only the fixings left visible. On going into the bathroom, we saw that the shower curtain was drawn around the bath. We both had the same thought and gingerly looked round the curtain. Phew! No bodies! The hallway was also stripped of mirrors and pictures.

When the decorator had finished his measurements and left, I went into the kitchen and demanded of the girl Michele what they thought they were doing. In here (where the pictures again had gone) were all the missing items stacked up on the floor of the dining area. A feeling of 'this isn't happening' was sweeping over me. It was like one of those dreams where you move from one absurd situation to another. For, apart from all my things, there were also their rucksacks and bags. Now, wouldn't you expect their bags and clothes to be in their respective bedrooms? Also, my mind registered, without counting them, about twelve pairs of matching white trainers laid out neatly in pairs in the middle of all this! Twelve pairs of trainers? They seemed to be all new and identical. Remember, they had only one rucksack and one holdall each AND they had brought their own bedding with them! What did they need twelve pairs of trainers for? By now I was so confused, ill and unable to cope and really didn't know how to handle this – this hasn't happened to most people before!

Michele ran from me through to the other girl, Adele, who did most of the talking in perfect English. She came off the phone and began to be most aggressive and rude. I said how they had no right to move things to such an extent and certainly not to remove all those items off the walls. She said,

"Oh yes, when we rent it becomes our home and we can do anything we like to it."

"Oh no, you can't," I said.

"Oh yes, we like to feel at home and as things were not 'feng shui' we had to move them! If you had not come in, you would not have known and when we leave, we put it all back."

"That is not the point," I said.

"Oh yes, that is the point," she said.

"No, it's not!"

Wait a minute, this conversation is going nowhere.

"Well," I said, "I want you to put everything back as it was and if there is any damage you will be liable."

In the corner of my eye, I could see through to the main bedroom.

"And why have you done that?"

The double bed had been moved to just inside the door and the covers were all lifted back to expose the bottom half of the mattress!

"Well, the mattress was damp."

"Did you wet it?" I asked.

"No," she asserted. "I am not the bebe!"

"Well, how was it damp?"

"You had a plastic cover on the mattress and under this it gets damp."

"Where from?" I enquired. "The cover is to protect it FROM moisture."

"From the ocean," she said (!). "The air is damp and so it needs to be exposed to dry off."

If the air is 'damp' surely, she was exposing the mattress to it and making it damp and anyway she had only 'exposed' half of it – what about the other half?

I left, and when I was home, I realised I was shaking and wasn't sure if it was the flu or the stress or both! I tossed and turned all that night and sweated and worried. Eventually at five a.m. a realisation swept over me. A thought had occurred. Actually, they had not damaged anything (as far as I know!) and, just maybe, they had done me a favour by taking down the wall hangings ready for the decorator! Well, I'm not going to tell them that, but I will tell them not to move the things back – I don't want them damaged, and they wouldn't remember where everything went and so to leave them alone.

However, my comforting thought did not last long because, a couple of days later, I had a phone call from an Irish man who was coming over with his fiancée to look for a house to buy as he was starting work at a local company and they would need a place to rent for two or three months. At that time of year this is exactly what you want as the tourist season is finished and you want a longer let. He said they would only be over for a couple of days, and could they come and view the apartment? Fine I said but I'll have to ask the people who are in it right now and arrange a time for you to see it.

I phoned the girls and explained the situation. Could I bring them in for five minutes when I come to collect the next week's rent anyway? When this happens, most people are quite happy to oblige. Not these girls!

"Oh no," one of them said. "You have already brought one person round – the decorator – and you do not have the right to bring more people in. It is invading our privacy and we do not like people looking at our things!" (After what they did to mine?)

Now this got me really worried again. Why did they

really not want this? After what they had done already you didn't know what they would do next. Drugs? Have the place cleared having already piled up the items? This now seemed all too suspicious.

"Well," I said. "Under the circumstances, I feel the apartment is not suitable for you – you don't like the way it was set up, you changed everything, and I now must ask you to leave at the end of the week."

"But we do like it, we just don't want strangers coming round."

Then she accused me of blackmailing her by saying let the people come round or get out! She started her aggressive attitude again by saying she would contact the tourist board and lawyers and that she was twenty-five years old and I would not talk to her mother like this—

"I would if she spoke to me like you are doing," I said.

In the end I hung up on her, as I had had to do every time I spoke with her on the phone.

The next day I lay in bed all day shivering and sweating alternately with my flu. Nevertheless, I spent a lot of time on the phone with the Tourist Board and the local Citizens Advice Bureau about how to handle the situation. The girls had referred to the rental agreement which we had both signed with the dates of the two weeks on it. This concerned me as to whether this bound me to the two weeks or because of the fact that they had only paid for one week I could put them out. The terms of the contract also stated that payment had to be made in full four weeks prior to the rental. This did not apply as they had arrived 'on spec' and also cancellation conditions did not apply.

From earlier conversations they had said they had stayed at Lochwinnoch, and so when I was speaking to the administration department of the tourist board, I suggested that we try to find out where that was. It was quite likely that they had found that place in the same brochure where they had found my place. Luckily there was only one place in that area and the owner there had indeed had a similar experience with them. They had had the same trouble with them that I had. The girls had dismantled one of the beds and put it in the wardrobe! Pictures were also removed from the walls. This lady had refused them an extended stay too. This was enough for the tourist board, the girls had upset two of their members and so the officer agreed to accompany me to make sure they left without trashing the place.

Meanwhile the girls were phoning the main Scottish Tourist Board who referred them to the local office. They went personally to that office to find out if I had the right to evict them. The poor girl behind the desk did not have the knowledge or the authority to tell them anything and so she phoned the administration department. The girls demanded to speak to them, but they refused and said they would see them on the Monday. Later I phoned the girls to insist they leave on the Monday and they started ranting again about how could I do this to the little children, where was my conscience and how could they do their good work if they had to keep moving house all the time. I told them that if they did not disrupt everywhere they went they would not have to move! A lot of their problem was that they did not ask first if they could move anything and when they were confronted about it, they became aggressive, abusive and started ranting and raving.

I met the tourist board officer on the Monday, and we went up to the apartment. The girl's bags were outside on the landing and when we went in to inspect lo and behold everything had been put back almost perfectly. They obviously had taken fright because of the official and decided to return the items despite the fact I had asked them not to.

As they stepped outside the official started to advise them about renting in Britain and what they should expect and how to respect the owner's property and this made them start off again! One of the girls began ranting demanding a copy of the rental agreement and she would get a lawyer involved and why was the official here anyway etc. etc. I had warned the officer not to get into an argument with them because of how they react but all she was trying to do was advise them of renting conditions and British ways. In the end we had to shut the door to stop the ranting.

"Well," said the officer, "now I see what you had to contend with, and I really saw what they were like – unbelievable! From such young girls too."

She then contacted the tourist information offices in the area to warn them in advance in case the girls turned up to book other accommodation.

I felt like we had been dealing with criminals but really, I think they were just two very strange people with weird and different ways – or were they? There were just too many inconsistencies.

Chapter 20

<u>Dogs</u>

To take dogs or not to take dogs? For one thing I have a cat and cats and dogs don't normally get on too well. I refused dogs for some years, but I was persuaded to take one by an owner who was almost pleading with me to accept her dog, a Chihuahua, very quiet, no shedding, well behaved, house-trained and they couldn't find anywhere else in the area, and it was getting late etc. etc.

    Reluctantly I agreed as it was small dog (smaller than a cat) and in fact all was well, no trouble at all. Petra, the Chihuahua, was obviously a baby substitute as it was carried in her arms a great deal. It had a cage which came with it into the room and this cage was cleaned with disinfectant which we could smell from outside the room. Petra WAS very quiet and sported several frilly outfits with matching hair ribbons! This little family made return visits quite a few times and I kept the cat out of sight of Petra as much as possible as Otto was really a bit bigger than the dog and twice as feisty!

    I did have a dog and cat incident when a large chocolate Labrador pushed open the lounge door one evening when Otto and I were in for the night watching TV with Otto lying on my knee, the dog saw the cat and a heavy chase ensued. When Otto saw the dog, he leapt vertically from my lap with loud hissing noises and literally flew towards the kitchen and escaped with the door closing behind him as it is a swinging two-way door. Phew! The dog almost banged into the door in his haste.

My rule for dogs is that they must not be left alone in the guest's room. One couple took a chance that I would not know it was there and went out to dinner. After a while the dog started barking. Oh no! I didn't want to open the door to comfort it in case it attacked me as it didn't know me! This was quite a big dog. I couldn't even call the owners as they didn't have a mobile phone and I didn't know which restaurant they had gone to. When the couple came back, I told them about the barking and she said, "Oh, that's unusual," almost as if I had done something to upset him. Not much of an apology but luckily, they were staying only one night. Thankfully there was no mess on the carpet or scratches on the door.

A different story from a young dog which was completely house trained according to its owner when booking in. It was a very lively and excited little fellow and that made me wonder if these statements would hold up.

When I did room service the following morning I saw a stain on the carpet, and it was a suspicious yellow colour. It was damp and on giving it the sniff test yes, sure enough I realised it was urine. Oh no! I cleaned it up as best I could, but the mark was not coming out. It needed a lot more deep-cleaning. When the owner came back, I pointed it out to him. He denied it was the dog saying he had spilled the water bowl and that's all it was. I said I was sorry, but I have a good sense of smell and that was not water. I said they would have to leave as I could not risk another accident.

That stain was very difficult to remove, and I had to get the professionals in. Even they could not get it out completely. I don't know why people can't say they are sorry and "He has never done that before" etc., etc., for example. Why lie about it? He would know that water would not stain a carpet.

Sometime later I reluctantly agreed to take a couple with a Collie and again I was assured that their dog was very well behaved, and elderly, so was quiet and slow.

What they didn't tell me was that it shed black hair copiously! When they left in the morning, I found that the white valance (or bed skirt as the Americans call it) was absolutely covered all the way round the bed in black hairs. It took me hours to get them off as the vacuum couldn't cope with them and so I had to use an extra sticky lint roller painstakingly strip by strip. Never again!

That was the last straw for me and dogs – no more!

Young Ones

Quite often neighbours and local people call upon us to put up their friends and relations for family gatherings and celebrations if they do not have enough space to host them themselves. This one time is notable for several reasons. The first, being that the grandparents who lived on the other side of town, were well known on the stage. They had chosen The Cherries from recommendations even though it meant the boys would have to be brought over in the car and collected again. Their grandson and friends were coming from Holland for four days on a visit. Fond Gran and Grandad told me what nice boys they were, well brought up etc., etc. (Well, why would I think otherwise but the older generation put great store on saying these things.)

The boys arrived – all in their early twenties – and went off happily to play golf as guests of their relatives to the famous Royal Troon Golf club. That night they wanted to know about coming in late should they go to a night club or something and I told them I would leave a key in the door for them. The first night they were in around eleven p.m. The second night was three a.m. but they were very quiet and even better they did not want to have breakfast. In the morning a girl rang for one of them and then again and left a message. I teased him about chasing the Scottish girls already and we had a good chat and laugh about it. The third morning around seven a.m. the phone rang, and it was a taxi driver asking if we had ordered a taxi in the name of – I said yes that name was staying here. I looked out the window and saw one of the boys waiting on the pavement. When the cab pulled up I saw him signal to a long haired blonde girl who came out from behind the hedge and climbed into the cab. He then returned to the house. Not what Grandma would have approved of!

I wondered whether to ignore it and pretend I didn't know and was tempted to turn a blind eye. Then I thought about how they were staying courtesy of the friend's grandparents I was upset for them and also, I could not condone what he had done and was angry at a girl perhaps being seen by the neighbours leaving the premises early in the morning. If that happened regularly then that certainly would damage MY reputation!

I decided to tackle the problem there and then and before the boy could settle back into his room I went along the corridor and knocked briefly on the door and went straight in! I was taking a gamble that he would be in that room as it was the relative who had the single and he and the other friend shared the twin room. I guessed that if he needed to be private, he would have changed rooms! Yes, I was right, there he was! He was very surprised to see me and looked distinctly guilty and sheepish! (It was hard at this point not to smile!) I told him off saying this was not a hotel and he was taking advantage of his friend's grandparent's generosity and that you did not do that sort of thing. Any extra guests would normally have to be paid for too. He tried to tell me that she had come in in the morning to say goodbye as she would not see him again. (Yes, she had come in, in the very early morning!) I also explained to him that I had to consider my own reputation.

    He apologised profusely and said he would bring no one else in. Yet again I saw the look of a naughty schoolboy caught in the act! No one appeared for breakfast – they were all too frightened of the dragon Mrs M!

    The mother, who was staying with the grandparents, phoned to say the boys would be collected at one p.m. At twelve-fifteen the same lad came down to the lounge where I was vacuuming and came up to me very gingerly and said what a mistake he had made and apologised again with his head down (naughty schoolboy again!). He said that he was normally a good person and that he was sorry he had so disrespected me and his friend and he really regretted it. He also said his friend knew nothing about it. Well, I didn't believe that as he had been using his room! I said I had had to speak to him as this was not a hotel and certainly not a house of ill repute! Then he said, "Well, nothing happened, but I'm really sorry again." (Oh yeah?) I told him I would not tell or charge his grandparents and when he went out the room I went through to the kitchen and laughed as silently as I could!

Disrespected? What was this? The Jerry Springer show in Ayrshire?

Chapter 21

The Nasties!

Since starting a B&B I have been very fortunate in not having had many guests who would definitely not be welcome again. I would say that ninety-five per cent or more are a joy and an entertainment. However, there have been one or two disturbing instances.

Now that many tourist offices have closed, B&Bs, when they are full, take it upon themselves more to pass on visitors to each other. This network works well both for visitors and accommodation providers alike. Sometimes, however, things go wrong. I had a referral call one night from a B&B about a mile away. They were full and could I take two couples. They wanted one or two nights and the B&B could only give them one night. Yes, I had two rooms available. They would come and inspect the premises. They arrived in a large Mercedes. The women came to inspect the rooms. Sometimes men just have to do as they are told! The women saw the rooms and said they wanted two double rooms. I had said I had a double and a twin. The twin is not ensuite but shares two bathrooms with only one single room which was not booked at this time. They immediately started haggling over the price. I stuck to the price of the ensuite but took a couple of pounds off the twin price. They said they might stay two nights so how much would that be? They went to consult with the husbands and came back with the husbands saying they would take the two nights but while they were out consulting, I had gone to check my bookings and saw I only had one night available anyway! One of the husbands then said, "Well, we want the lower price as it's not our fault you can't take us for the two nights." That is actually back to front as two nights might be cheaper than one, not the other way round. I suppose he really meant he wanted the lower price although they were staying just one night. Perhaps stupidly, I reluctantly agreed. The women then asked if I could give them some sandwiches as they didn't want to go for a meal. Again, stupidly, I agreed. I had no ham as requested but offered tuna.

"No."
"Cheese?"
"Yes."
"Chutney?"
"No."
"Mustard?"
"No."

Not once did anyone say thank you. They opted for cheese, no chutney. I said to one of the men, "I will only charge you £2 for the sandwiches." That was for all of them – was I crazy?

No response.

Off they went in their car without giving any indication as to when they wanted the sandwiches. I had assumed they wanted sandwiches because they were too tired to go out again.

The only cheese I had was my best camembert and I gave them some cherry tomatoes on the side. I put butter on my really nice granary bread. I wrapped each plate in cling film and set them on the dining table. They came back after nine p.m. and I asked them if they wanted the sandwiches then or to take away for tomorrow's lunch. No, they were coming in now. I made a pot of tea and took it through. I was watching TV in the lounge area, but I could see two of them reflected in the window. One of the men opened up a sandwich and peeled it apart and made a face of disgust. My best camembert! He didn't even taste it and there then ensued a very hushed conversation probably about the sandwiches and being charged. I couldn't hear what they were saying due to my slight deafness and their strong Irish accents! When they had finished the tea, they came through and said good night. The guy who had done the peeling came over to me and put his hand on my arm and said, "We didn't like your sandwiches!"

"Oh dear," I said, "it was my best camembert!"

Off they went upstairs.

As I have only one dining table, I like to stagger the breakfasts as not everyone likes to share a table with strangers (although some guests love meeting new people).

That morning, I had one single guy (he's another story!) and these two couples. The single guy wanted breakfast at eight thirty a.m. and the others at nine a.m. Perfect. At eight forty-five one of the couples appeared, helped themselves to cereal and sat down at the table which was clearly set for four and the other guest was still there. They said the milk jug was not big enough for them. It was for the single man. I took through their larger jug and did the pleasantries about the bad weather that day (what a shame!) all to stony faces. I ignored this, and kept smiling (it's hard going sometimes being polite!). The single guy escaped, and as the second couple appeared as I cleared his things away, I said, "We have an overlap this morning." (Hint, hint.) I served the first couple the full cooked option as ordered. It was looking really tasty and perfectly cooked, and I had added some black pudding which I usually only have on request as most people don't like it. (Why am I doing this, I'm never going to win these people round!)

One of the women asked if I had any cocoa.

"Yes," I said. "Would you like hot chocolate?"

"Yes, I don't take tea." Why didn't she ask for it when ordering the night before?

I served the next couple. The first man demanded more white toast (no please then?).

All four left half their breakfasts.

The first couple came to pay – no money for the sandwiches. They said they had never been asked to pay for sandwiches anywhere else and they always ask for them. They said they couldn't eat them as there was something strange in them (wish there had been!) mayo or something. (Is mayo strange?)

"No," I said, "I did not put anything strange on them, just slices of a very good camembert."

"Well, he (the first rude man) tasted it and warned us not to touch it." (Haven't you minds of your own?)

"Oh," she said, "and I didn't get a wink of sleep last night as the alarm clock had beeped every hour."

"Oh dear," I said and tried not to smile and apologised and said she should have put it outside the room somewhere but thank you for telling me, I will look into it.

The other woman came to pay and said the lights by the

bed weren't working and there was nothing on the TV.

"Why didn't you tell me?" I said. "You should always tell the owner if you have a problem, and they will fix it for you."

They stomped off and I called the other B&B to warn them as they were then going there for the second night. When told the story of the sandwiches the owner said, "Well they won't get any here!"

As for the bedside lights, someone had pulled out the plug and so wouldn't you check that to see why it wasn't working? Nothing was wrong with the TV. They clearly were just 'at it'!

I subsequently heard that they did not arrive at the other B&B at all and didn't have the courtesy to tell them. Probably knew I would be telling them. How can people be like that? They always asked for sandwiches to save on meals out and I'm sure they hoped that their hosts would not charge them. To do these things deliberately is quite shocking and I wonder if they took pleasure in it. They didn't seem to and must lead a rather miserable life.

Chapter 22

A Referral

As they were full that night a B&B in the town centre called to see if I could take a youngish girl that night. The owner obviously had no idea that this girl had a problem. Because she was a referral, I took her in but it wasn't long before I had suspicions about her. For one thing she had no luggage. Then she said she had no money but that her husband was arriving from Glasgow later and he would pay when he arrived. She then stayed in her room (presumably I thought) to wait for him. It was a Sunday this day and we were having a family visit from relatives. While entertaining them, time went on, and later on in the afternoon I thought I should check on her, and see if she had heard from her husband. I knocked on her door and got no reply. I called her name – no response. Then I tried the door and found that it was locked. Oh dear. I knocked and knocked and called her repeatedly until eventually I heard a drowsy response. She came to the door and then I could see that she was obviously under the influence of drink or drugs or both. She was, as some would say, 'Out of her face!' I told her that if her husband did not arrive within half an hour, I would have to ask her to leave. Then I gave her my phone as she didn't seem to have one and told her to call him and get him to call me. She rudely shut the door and I heard her turning the key. After the half hour with no response or call from the husband I enlisted the help of my brother-in-law who knocked and shouted through the door that we were now going out and that she would have to leave. We would take her back down to the town and she could wait for her husband there and if she didn't come out, we would call the police. She did come out thankfully and we took her to the station to wait for her fictitious, or not, husband. We never did find out where she was from or if indeed there was a husband.

On our return, I checked her room and saw she had used a cup and it looked as if she had just laid on the bed not gone into it. I straightened everything up and prepared it for the next visitor. This turned out to be a customs and excise guy who was staying for one night. At breakfast the next morning he said he had something to show me. He had used the single bed and found an empty half bottle of vodka under the pillow!

"OMG!" I said in horror. "I'm so sorry," and told him about the girl.

"Don't worry," he said. "I could tell that the bed hadn't been slept in so it wasn't a problem."

Lesson to learn – don't assume a bed hasn't been "used"!

The next day I called the other B&B to see if they knew anything about the girl, but they didn't. She had just turned up at their door asking for a room. As they were full, she had called me. She had not noticed that the girl had no luggage and assumed she had come by car.

Mother and Dancer Daughter

I had a call from a mother who wanted a room for herself and her daughter who was competing in a junior Scottish Country

Dance championship in the town. They were staying that night in a town three miles away and wanted to be nearer for the next night. I booked them in, and they said they would arrive between noon and one p.m. Two p.m., three p.m., four p.m., five p.m. came and went with no sign of them nor were there any messages. I phoned the number she had called me from but it went to the answer machine message. I left a message to call me, and I also called a place in the town where they might have been staying the previous night but no, they had not been there.

Later on that night, I had an enquiry from a couple who wanted a twin room but because of the mother and daughter and it being a very busy weekend I had only two single rooms left. There was an extra folding bed in one of the single rooms but I explained that there would not be much walking space in that room for two adults and so they opted for the two single rooms. This meant that I had to take out the folding bed and put back the armchair which normally sits there.

When this couple arrived and no sign of the mother and daughter, I offered them the larger twin room instead. This was gratefully accepted.

At ten p.m. I heard someone coming to the front door. When I opened the door, I saw a young girl about thirteen years of age standing there saying nothing. Mother was speaking to the taxi driver. Yes, this was the mother and daughter! No apology was offered, and she seemed quite miffed that I had given their room away. She said that her phone had no signal and had not got my message. When I said they could have the two single rooms the girl seemed quite frightened and ran to mum. This led to a discussion whether to stay or go back to the town. The taxi was waiting to hear what they were doing. Eventually I said I could put a folding bed in one of the rooms. They decided on that, and I showed them into the lounge, put on the TV for them and went to do the bed. Out with the armchair again, in with the folding bed, then I had to find sheets and a duvet. I DON'T NEED THIS! I showed them up to the room and asked what time they would like breakfast.

"How late can you do it?"

"Nine a.m.?" (I was going out that morning.)

"HOW late? You finish at nine a.m.?"

Well, we agreed on nine thirty a.m. and then there were decisions about what they would have for breakfast. The daughter kept shrugging her shoulders in typical teenage style. Order taken, I asked if they would like some milk for a cuppa.

"No."

I went off to bed and was half undressed when I heard the mother going downstairs. With no car to go to she must be looking for something. I re-dressed and followed her down. She had put on the lights which I had put off. When I reached her, she said, "I need milk." No 'Sorry to disturb you' or 'could I possibly?'

"I thought you didn't want any," I said, not too graciously. I was becoming more annoyed now.

When I brought her the usual small sized jug she asked, "Is that enough for cereal?"

"Sorry?"

"She wants cereal," and picks up a bowl from the breakfast table. "|We have cereal, just need milk."

No 'Could I?' or 'Would you mind?'

In the morning they joined the breakfast table where one gentleman was finishing up. I came in and breezily asked, "How are you this morning?"

"Still tired," said mother with a 'torn face.'

I ignored that and said to the guy to break the ice for them.

"This is a champion dancer we have here," hoping that would please the daughter and she might just raise a smile. No.

I went through to the kitchen to get the coffee and I heard the guy making small talk about the dancing. The girl was saying nothing as usual and mother answered in monosyllables.

When I took in the coffee mother said she liked hot milk (with her cornflakes).

"Sorry?"

"Would you have a small jug of hot milk?"

I nearly said 'What's the magic word?'

"I'll get that for you," I managed.

When taking in the mother's scrambled egg, I noticed that the daughter had barely touched her cornflakes and had spilled a lot on the tablecloth. She may be a champion dancer but her social skills have not arrived yet!

Mother asked me to put her coffee cup in the microwave to warm it up. Her manner really was quite atrocious! It was very hard for me to keep the smile going here!

I asked where they had stayed the night before (so I could phone and ask if they had been asked to leave!). She said the name of a large hotel and said it was very good and very reasonable only charging them £40 for the room. Well, that had been my price too for a single room with an extra bed so I hoped there would be no argument or complaint on leaving. Thankfully there wasn't although they did not leave until eleven thirty a.m.

Another mother and daughter from Ireland were here for the Highland Dancing Championship another year and when they left, I discovered that the daughter had obviously not bathed or showered before going to bed as the sheets were absolutely covered in dark make up from the tanning cream she had used for the competition. That was very difficult to wash out. Would they do that at home too? They must have known that that was going to happen, but I suppose they didn't care, as it was not they who would have to clean the sheets! No apologies naturally.

Chapter 23

A Tail to Tell!

Even my four-legged friend Otto the cat makes a contribution to these tales.

He was only one year old and already had used up some of his nine lives. The name Otto comes from our street name – Ottoford Crescent. Otto, King of the Road. Unfortunately, he was more like 'Wimp of the Street'! He had two black circles on one of his white back legs so we thought of calling him 'Buttons' but Otto seemed to suit him better.

When he was old enough at six weeks of age to be allowed out on his own, he was continually being beaten up and intimidated by the local older tabby cat whom we christened 'The Bully'. We could see him being challenged by this cat and when chased he would lie down on his back in the submission position. I would chase off the Bully, bring in Otto telling him that this was his garden and not to be such a wimp. As Otto grew, he gradually became full size and was now actually bigger than The Bully. Now The Bully did not come round when Otto was there! Not only that, but he, Otto, also gave me a good laugh one day when he was sitting on the pavement outside our gate. Next door to us lived a couple of West Highland Terriers. They were just coming out for a walk when they spied Otto sitting there. They started to run and give chase but instead of running away Otto stood still not moving with a look on his face which said 'OK, what's your game then?' If he had had hands they would have been on his hips! The dogs didn't know what to do and did a complete 'Tom and Jerry' screech to a stop and then made little whining noises. Then Otto turned and stalked off with his head and tail in the air! I wished I'd had a video of that!

Then, one day, he came in and Lorna said, "Oh, Mum, Otto's lost some of his tail!" Sure enough, a third of his tail was missing and looked like it had been chewed off. The vet said either he had caught it on something and had to chew it free or a fox or something had done it. A big vet bill followed for a small op to repair it. Subsequently, he went around with a shaved three-inch end to his tail which looked so strange. A few months later he developed a lump on his side which the vet said was his liver all distended maybe due to infection or being kicked. Yet another vet bill for treatment.

The next happening was the most serious. On a very wet and windy day he did not appear for lunch or supper. This was a most unusual occurrence as his appetite was legendary. By evening we knew something was wrong. At nine thirty p.m., during a very bad storm I heard him yowling outside. I opened the window to a blast of rain and wind on my face and saw the most pathetic sight. Otto was lying straddled on the stone planter where he usually jumped on to the window ledge to ask to come in. He was braying a deep throated sound with huge saucer eyes and was desperately saying 'Help me, help me!' I hated to think how long he had been struggling home or where he had come from. He couldn't stand and his back end was totally limp. I knew he was seriously hurt. I ran round to the back door and lifted him gently. He was purring as if to say, "Thank God, I'm home!"

I phoned the emergency vet immediately and he was wonderful saying, "Bring him to the surgery and I'll be there in five minutes." Oh, to have the same service for humans!

He took him home with him to keep an eye on him as he said Otto was too shocked to x-ray that night. He gave him strong painkillers and said to phone in the morning. The diagnosis was a broken pelvis probably sustained in a car accident. He would not operate on him, but we were to keep him confined and on pain relief for up to six weeks.

I had to keep him in the kitchen in a cage for the six weeks and that was stressful for both of us. He was desperate to get out and escaped a couple of times complaining bitterly when he was captured and put back inside.

Once he was able to be released, he had to wear an 'Elizabethan collar' round his head to prevent him licking the back area. He would clack off walls and furniture and although that was comical, it was not funny for him. The guests made a big fuss of him, but he would much rather have been outside hunting. Soon the collar was off, but he still had a sensation down his left side, and he would lick himself to the point of having a bare patch on his side which then became raw and infected. After many medications and creams and having the collar back on many times I decided it was time to try something else. I had the idea of putting a coat on him but there are no coats for cats and dog coats just sit on the back. I needed something that would cover the hip area and was tight enough to prevent him from licking at it. After hours of trying to come up with an idea along with friends thinking too, I suddenly thought (in the middle of the night, as you do) a baby grow! This could cover the area but still could have the tail out of the popper studs! Now, trying to dress a cat is not the easiest of things to do and I asked a friend if she would hold him for me while I put it on. I bought long gardening gloves for us both and I picked him up with nice soothing noises and we petted him a little. I'm certain he had a suspicious look on his face! Getting one paw down a sleeve was enough!

"Oh, no, you don't!" said the furry protest and the struggle began. After loud yowlings and flying claws, we had to give up and off he shot with the baby grow trailing behind him and us having several scratches dripping blood! Well, that went well!

Back to the drawing board! The next attempt was an elasticated 'skirt' which covered his back end. This worked partially and the vet assistant called him the cat with the 'tutu'. Unfortunately, it came off too easily and so then I tried to attach it to his neck collar but now he could reach under it to lick, cats being real contortionists.

I then enlisted the help of a friend in Glasgow who obtained some black stretchy material, and we designed a shape which had stretch elastic round the back legs and covered his back then was sewn on to the neck collar. I managed to put it on him while he was eating, and it was hilarious seeing him kick out his back legs trying to get it off. It stayed firm very well and as it didn't really annoy him after he got used to it. He wore it quite happily and did not try to lick – amazing. The only problem was that when he was outside, he would come home many times minus the coat AND collar! There must be countless numbers of coats/collars around the neighbourhood and trees. Either that or someone saw him and thought that was a shame dressing up a cat and released him from it. The minute he had the coat off he was back licking again. I had the sewing machine up permanently in the kitchen. He, of course, was a great topic of conversation with the guests who had never seen a cat with a coat on before! He was also featured on the front page of the local newspaper. It took two years of coat wearing before he suddenly stopped licking and has been fine ever since. Having watched the programme Dragon's Den on TV I'm sure there is a niche market for this product! All cats and dogs would benefit from not having to wear the very uncomfortable plastic head covers. Trouble is I don't have the ability to set that up! Maybe I should contact Deborah Meaden! (Joking!)

Naughty Otto!

Otto is a complete opportunist! Too intelligent for his own good!

When I'm cooking in the kitchen I shut the conservatory door, which is off the kitchen, and keep Otto away from stealing the bacon, sausages etc. This worked well for a long time – until I had a cat flap put in on the conservatory door for his access to the garden.

Quite often when I'm cooking, I see the guests going to and fro to their cars as they load up for their departure. This day was one of those days. When I went through to greet the guests with my usual bright and breezy, "Good morning, did you sleep well?"

One of the women said, "Oh, em, Margaret, I was just wondering – do you think, maybe, that the cat, maybe, has been up on the table, at the butter?"

I looked at the butter dish. In horror I saw that there was an undeniable evidence of cat activity! The butter was halfway off the dish on to the table cover and it had obvious lick marks on it! Oh no!

"Oh, I'm so, so sorry, I do apologise," I gabbled, blushing furiously as I quickly removed the offending mess. (Good job there weren't any cat hairs in the milk jug!) I quickly brought in a fresh dish of butter and made a note to myself to in future use a lidded butter dish and place a fancy cover over the milk jug!

I realised that Otto must have gone out through his cat flap, round the house to the front and spied the front door open as the people were out at their car and rushed in in glee knowing what would be on the table in the dining room!

I explained what must have happened (carefully didn't say it was their fault for leaving the front door open!) and they laughed and said that they had cats too and that is how they knew!

Thank goodness because if they had not liked cats that would have been very serious, and they could have given us bad reviews and requests for a refund!

There once was a woman who gave me a fright. I was cooking breakfast and went through to the dining room to serve a porridge order and as I came through the swing door, I saw this woman standing spread-eagled against the wall in the corner of the room behind her chair. Her eyes were huge, and she was rigid! "Get it away, get it away," she shouted when she saw me.

"What, what?" I said looking around for a tarantula at least or a mouse even. Then I spied a tail visible under the table. Otto shot through the open door into the kitchen!

"She's terrified of cats," said her companion.

"Sorry about that," I said soothingly. "I'll make sure he keeps away." Again, he must have come in the front door! Don't you think someone like that would ask whether there was a cat where they were going to stay or at least ask when they arrived so that I could have kept him away?

Chapter 24

<u>Jammies</u>

Not only could Otto be a problem, but I too can cause myself a problem. I have the breakfast routine down to a fine art. I get up forty-five minutes before the first breakfast is due giving me enough time to wash, dress, apply minimal makeup and get breakfast cooked and ready. The table is set the night before and orders are requested so that there is no waiting time for them in the morning. In twenty years, I have only ever had one person who refused to order the night before as she said she didn't know what she would want in the morning and so she would tell me then.

My alarm clock is usually very reliable although most days I haven't needed it as my body clock wakes me in good time.

One morning I awoke at five thirty a.m. and couldn't get back to sleep. By about six fifteen a.m. I nodded off and when I woke next the alarm was ringing and it was seven thirty a.m. – the time for the first breakfast! Had the alarm been ringing since six forty-five a.m. or had I forgotten to set it?

I shot out of bed, and as I was wearing grey pyjamas, I thought they'll just have to think they are grey jogging trousers. I put on a pink gilet over my top, did a quick hair brush, and rushed down to the kitchen. Ten minutes later I'm saying, "Good morning, how are you? Did you sleep well?" as if everything was perfectly normal! The guest was a man on his own who was busy on his iPad and he obviously didn't twig what I was wearing or care! Phew! I just had time to quickly wash and dress before the next guests descended for breakfast.

Me Again!

I was waiting for the arrival of four men coming here for golf from Sweden and who were arriving on the late flight due in at one a.m. I don't usually accept bookings with arrivals as late as this because if the flight is delayed then it is too late to stay up for that. These men had wanted to stay a few days and so I reckoned that was worth staying up for. I had stupidly gone to lie on my bed (fully clothed) to read until they arrived. The flight was delayed and of course I nodded off! My bedroom door was wide open so that I could hear the front doorbell. I can't have actually heard the doorbell for the first thing I knew I awakened hearing voices coming up the stairs. Aargh! As I came to, I saw them looking straight at me as they came to the top of the stairs! I felt completely naked (though I wasn't of course) and got up blushing furiously. They were laughing but very nice and apologising for their plane being delayed. I showed them to their rooms then happily went back to bed. This time I could not get back to sleep! I think I'm quite glad that those late flights no longer run.

Why Did the Woman NOT Cross the Road?

Yes, me again!

I had been caring now and again for an elderly lady, Mary, who lived in the ground floor flat in a building where I used to live on the top floor. I had kept in contact with her when I moved as we had become friends and I would do her shopping for her now and again. She was so independent that when asked how she was she would always say, 'Fine, Margaret' and that she didn't need anything. She never wanted to 'be a burden on anyone.' She had never had any children and had no family apart from a niece who lived a couple of hours away and could not visit often because she herself had an extremely disabled brother to care for. Mary had a brother, but he was even older than Mary and could not help her much either. The neighbours in the building had changed over the years and had not got to know her as she was next door with a separate door entrance.

Mary had many stories of her life and was a wonderful source of information on so many subjects and also kept up to date with world news and really was far more aware of the world than most people and her memory was phenomenal. She could recite Robert Burns, McGonagall, Shakespeare and many more. She even had poems she had made up herself and had many jokes in her repertoire. Considering her age and how physically frail she was she was amazing and tremendously entertaining.

She and her husband had been collecting antiques for years and her flat was absolutely full of amazing items. Every space on every wall was covered in pictures and paintings, one of which was a Lowry print. Although a print it was still worth a goodly sum. Many pictures were obviously old and valuable and memorable and she had a couple of paintings of Glasgow depicting the old tramcars on the city streets.

There were several glass cabinets of figurines and valuable porcelain and china and even ivory pieces.

On one of my visits, she asked me if I checked my coins and bank notes every time I went shopping?

"No, other than to check my change," I replied. "Why?"

"Oh," she said. "You must as there is valuable currency out there. Not old either, as you might think, but of limited editions commemorating events, people, places or battles." She then told me to go into her safe which was well hidden in a cupboard and find a long sock... Sure enough there was an old sock full of cash, mainly 50p and £1 coins. They were all in commemoration of people or events e.g., Beatrix Potter, Olympic Games of several years, The Great Exhibition, The Battle of Britain, Benjamin Britten, Winston Churchill, Peter Rabbit even. She also had an album full of the coins in the separate leaves.

As I held all these coins in my palm having heard some of the value I said to her, "Mary, do you realise I am holding about £20,000 in my hand?"

"Yes," she said. "I've been collecting for years now."

"And just from change you got while shopping?"

"Yes."

"Wow, I must start looking!"

Next, she said that there was a valuable Jane Austen £5 note which has not yet been found (unless someone has it and not revealed its whereabouts.) There were only four of these printed apparently with the small head of Jane Austin underneath her large head on the notes. The normal Jane

Austen notes do not have this little head. Three of these notes have been found but the fourth is still somewhere at large. This now is worth a cool £50,000 if you find it. Start checking your £5 notes!

She also said that if you go on eBay you will see lots of coins for sale. Not that they all sell for the prices asked but some do, depending on their rarity value.

One day I was excited to find a Beatrix Potter 50p coin in my change. I Googled it only to find out that there are many different Beatrix Potter coins, not all valuable. Mine was worth a paltry £1.50 but I have kept it anyway.

"What are you going to do with them?" I asked Mary.

"Oh, nothing," she said. "I just like collecting them."

Some coins and notes have errors in the printing or are slightly misshapen and this makes them extra valuable. One coin has the queen's head facing the wrong way. How many people would ever notice that?

Good job she has a locked safe in the house!

In addition to the walls being covered, every table and piece of furniture and even window ledges are laden with beautiful china, table lamps, figures, vases, intricate ornaments of all kinds. Far from being a clutter of old junk, her flat is an Aladdin's cave of history and beautiful items.

It is her health that is Mary's problem. She had had a triple heart bypass a few years ago but had never really recovered from it. She has skin cancer and suspected internal cancers too. She has other conditions too resulting in a lack of appetite and nausea and so was losing weight as a result. She collapses now and again, and one day when I was with her, she was sitting on a kitchen chair as I was doing some dishes for her and I heard her making some groaning noises. I turned round and she was holding her head in her hands. I went to her and when I said we should call an ambulance I heard her softly agreeing. I knew then she was bad. Two hours later they came and took her to hospital but because of COVID-19 restrictions I could not go with her. I just tidied up and went home. Happily, she was back home in a few days.

On one of my visits, I had a scary experience of a different kind.

It was a very cold winter's day with rain and very high winds. Her building is right on the sea front and so gets the full force of the storms. I had parked across the small road on the sea front as the landward side was fully occupied with residents' cars. I opened the car door and had it almost wrenched out my hand. It was also hard to push the door shut again. I hoped that on my return the wind would have died down a bit as I had difficulty keeping my feet. I stayed all afternoon bringing her tea (she was mainly bed bound at that time and she had given me the entry code) and chatting then I made her meal in the evening. Her flat was full of food in the fridge and freezer and her kitchen cupboards had dozens of tins and packets which had been bought over the years. Because of a lack of appetite, they have not been used much. I took some to the food bank for her.

She did have a carer coming in previously but as soon as she was able to cope marginally well, she let them go saying that 'there are other people who need them more than I do'. Now she needed them again, but it takes time to organise.

So, there I was having made the homemade soup she liked and a tasty snack for afters. She would eat if it was made for her but could not face it on her own.

I had to leave her as I had a B&B guest booked in and had to get back for him arriving.

I thought that the wind had died down a bit but on leaving I saw that it had merely changed direction and was actually worse with seventy mph+ gusts and more. I could hardly stand, never mind cross the road! I edged along the building to the corner where there was a narrow inset to partially shelter me. I waited to see if there would be a break in the gusts when I could make a run for it. It was only crossing a small road after all with my car opposite me. I soon began to realise that that was not going to happen. The bags I was carrying were being blown out horizontally from me. What was I going to do? I saw a car or two coming towards me, but they turned into a side street. I waved manically and shouted, "Help, help!" but my voice disappeared in the wind. I could hardly hear it myself. I was wearing a white jacket in the dark but clearly no one could see me or if they did, they would think I was waving to someone else. Panic was beginning to grip me.

A thought came to me that I could go to the next door along from Mary's and ring the bell of the guy on the top floor and ask if he could see me across the road. This is the door to the entrance of where I used to live. At this point I didn't care if I was perceived as a very old person! I knew him from years of living in the building, so I edged back along the wall to the next door and pressed his name button. After three tries, I eventually realised with a sinking feeling that he wasn't in. There was no point in ringing the other resident's bells as I knew that they were all single women like me so would not be able to help. Well, now what? Should I ring the police? There is no police station in the town anymore because of cutbacks so it would take some time for them to come even if they could. Next, I thought of trying the local taxi company. I had my phone, and I knew the number from many years of calling them for guests. They knew me so I thought they might help. I got out my phone and rang and when they answered I shouted my problem. The woman on the other end said she could not hear me because of the wind!

I had to edge my way along the wall again to go into Mary's storm doors and rang again. That was better, but she said no one could come because if anything happened to me, then they would be responsible, and their insurance would not cover it. "Whaat? Well, what can I do?" I asked her.

She told me to order a cab and I would have to get into the taxi and pay the minimum fare. Just to cross the street!

"OK, OK," I said in desperation. "Please send one round." In about ten minutes the cab arrived, and I got in with difficulty as again the wind was whipping the door out of my hands.

"Where are you going?" he asked.

"Did you hear about my problem?" I asked.

"You need to go to your car? Where is it?"

"That's it right there across the street but I can't get to it without being blown over."

Without a murmur he started the car and manoeuvred it to the other side of the small road.

I said that I would pay him in the car as it would blow away when I got out. I was expecting that he would say 'No, no, don't be silly just be safe' but he took the money! Then he opened his door with difficulty and opened mine and took my arm and helped me five steps to my car. Then he had to lean on my door to close it.

Phew! I won't forget that night but I'm sure it would have given him a story to tell his colleagues.

I was totally unimpressed with that service but at least I had reached my car which was actually rocking in the wind but thankfully it started, and I got back home where it was much more sheltered, and I was in time for my arriving guest!

Another Very Strong Character

Jean came here taking a single room for a month at a time year after year. She lived on the outskirts of London but was Scottish by birth. She came north each year for a holiday as she felt at home here. She had never married and now had no family anywhere nearby. We bonded very well, and I would take her when I was going out and I would take her on trips which I thought she would like, and it was company for me too when I was not too busy.

After a number of years, she decided to re-locate here and she bought an apartment in an over 60s facility where she would have her meals provided, help at night if needed, and the company of mostly single people like herself.

After she moved, she changed her bank to the local branch here in the town. She was sent a cheque book which was fine but then they had the audacity to send her a debit card and a credit card! She had never had cards before and was outraged that she had been sent them without being asked if she wanted them! I tried to explain to her that most people had them now as it saved them carrying a lot of money around but oh no, she wasn't having any of that.

"But are you not afraid you might get mugged?" I asked.

"No, I think I could handle them," she insisted.

Oh dear, I could just imagine her trying to knee any attacker! She just would not be convinced of the danger she could be in.

She marched down to the bank and slapped the cards on the counter and said, "You can have these back I don't want them and did not ask for them! I've used cash and the occasional cheque all my life and that suits me fine." The teller tried to explain how useful they are and how to use them. Jean wasn't having any of it saying again, "I don't want them and I couldn't remember any such pin or whatever you call it—"

At which point the teller broke in, saying, "But you create a pin number you can remember like a birthday or a special number only you would remember—"

"No, you are not listening to me – I don't want them!"

Then she marched out again having fastened up her bag minus the cards!

Another time she had a ding-dong at a local fruit shop. She wanted some apples and tomatoes and could not find any UK ones.

"Where are your British apples and tomatoes?" she asked.

"Sorry," said the assistant, "we only have French and Dutch ones in just now."

"Let me speak to the manager," said Jean.

The poor manager was then subjected to a long spiel about using British produce and supporting local businesses to stop them going out of business. She ended by saying that she would never shop there again until their policy was changed!

I'm sure Jean kept all the staff and residents where she lived in order and probably a few of the more timid ladies, were a bit in awe and fear of her! I do know that the staff actually loved her!

While I was away one year, she moved herself into a care home as she felt she needed more help. Unfortunately, she did not check on the condition of the other residents before she moved. It turned out that none of them were mentally able to have a conversation and so Jean stayed in her room most of the time. When she was shown round the home, she was not told that the place was not suitable for her. She certainly should have been, and I was so angry about that. She didn't feel she could move again.

She did go for walks by herself and liked crosswords and I visited frequently, and we had her over for Christmas etc. but it was a lonely life for her. She only lasted two years in that place before she sadly died.

Chapter 25

My Availability

People often say to me, "Are you not tied to the house doing B&B?"

No, I tell them, a thing I love about this business is that you can do it if and when you want to. If you want to go out somewhere one night and you don't have any bookings listed then you can put no vacancy on the website for that date. If the tourist office calls for a guest and gets no reply, they will just call the next place. Nowadays it's likely that the calls will come through on the mobile phone too so you can deal with that by recommending anyone you know who has a vacancy. The mobile is useful also for accepting a booking for that night if you are out and about whereas before mobiles you would miss bookings if a call came when you were out. For your own holidays you just block off the days that you need.

Having said that, there are occasional times when all that doesn't work. If you have forward bookings and nearer to the time you find that there is somewhere you need to be and you must go then you think, 'What can I do?' If I could get the guests into another B&B nearby, I would explain to the guests the situation and they would be quite happy with that and thank me for rebooking them.

One time I had no options available. Fortunately, I had a

phone number for the guest (it is essential to get an address and phone number for all guests when they contact you) and I left the key under a stone as the guy had been before and I knew he would be fine. He was quite chuffed actually that I trusted him enough to do that and anyway I was coming back the next day.

Another time I had a problem as I had guests coming in from South Africa and I could not contact them. I was so fortunate that in the circumstances a very good friend, (who had never done B&B) agreed to take over for me for a few days – the proviso being she would not do a cooked breakfast!

The family who arrived were wonderful at accepting that and they even managed to persuade her to do simple things like egg on toast or a bacon sandwich! My friend loved the children and even bought a racket and ball and played with them at French cricket in the back garden and then got a football out of the garage and played with that with them. The family were charmed with her, and I wasn't missed at all! Great!

There was only one time when I could not reach a guest as his phone was not switched on and I had to leave a note on the front door telling him that due to unforeseen circumstances he was booked into another guest house and here was the address, name and directions. He too was ok with it and not perturbed at all. Did I say that almost all B&B guests are lovely?

Internet Dating

What, you might think, has internet dating got to do with B&B? Interesting question!

I had a call from a lady who lived about three miles away and she wanted to book in a single guy. When I asked his name she said, 'Alan' and then laughed as she said she wasn't sure of his second name as it was 'Baldy' – maybe a different spelling? She was going to meet him on a date from the internet and she wondered if this was his pseudonym or whether his mother had a sense of humour! "OK..."

He was coming up on business from Manchester and was going to meet up with her. (I don't think I would have been telling all this to a stranger!) When you think about it why did he not book in himself? Well, she was the local one, but he could have done it surely?

Anyway, he arrived, driving a very nice BMW and was good looking as well. Nice one, I thought, but I hope he likes talkative women! I did not, of course, let on that I knew of his arrangements.

When he left for his date, there was a strong smell of aftershave in the house! I grinned to myself. I wondered when he would come back – early if it went wrong? Late if he had found 'the one'? Not at all that night?

At breakfast the next day he asked whether he had locked the door properly and I said, "Oh yes, that was fine – I didn't hear you come in. Were you very late?" (Nosy, nosy...) "Oh, about 12.30 a.m.," he said.

OK... (I didn't ask).

I let him have his breakfast in peace but when he was paying his bill, I just had to ask him the question!

"How did the date go?"

I wondered if he would be embarrassed but the woman must have told him she had told me because he replied smiling, "I wondered when that would come up!"

He did go a bit pinkish but chatted quite happily about how he had been married over twenty years and it was difficult starting again especially as he travels a lot. I asked him if he would see her again and he said he probably would. I restrained myself from saying, "Well, if it doesn't work out you know where I am!"

Date Night

It's interesting to observe people's relationships and interactions with each other. Unmarried people are always trying to impress each other and create laughter and generally work at having a good time and also, they smile a lot. Apart from being on their phones they do smile and talk to each other. I generalise of course!

Married couples are usually much quieter and as they know each other so well they do not talk nearly as much. After all, they have said so much over the years they are comfortable with each other and know that they do not have to impress any more. As women enjoy talking about almost anything they tend to be much more communicative than the men. Women will tell you their life stories sometimes the minute they come in the door!

For one couple this was definitely not the case! He booked them in by phone late one afternoon. He gave a perfectly normal name and time of arrival. When they arrived, he was pleasant although not chatty and she said not very much at all. 'Hello' was about the length of her conversation and actually looked a bit uncomfortable. I couldn't help but see that they were both wearing what were obviously business suits. They went into their room, and I noticed that neither of them had any luggage. Were they going to go back out to the car and get it? I was now busy in the kitchen preparing my evening meal and the window looks on to the driveway. Nobody came out. Ah ha, I thought! I also had the feeling that I had seen the guy before somewhere although I did not know him. He was quite distinctive looking and I really wondered where I recognised him from.

They had ordered an early breakfast (presumably going back to work) and the next day the woman really seemed quite uncomfortable as at the breakfast table (same clothes as the day before!) she didn't say a word and kept her head down every time I went in to see if they required anything. He tried to talk normally, and I thought again, "I know that face!"

I hadn't asked them to sign the Visitors' Book when they arrived the night before (always a cardinal sin for a B&Ber but I was too busy wondering about them!) and so when they had finished their breakfast I asked if they would and apologised for forgetting the protocol.

"Certainly," he said, and they went into their room to get ready to leave. As I was saying goodbye to them, I again noticed the lack of luggage. When they had left and gone out of the driveway I went to the book and – no, they hadn't!

It was actually only a few days later while I was watching TV, I saw him! He was being interviewed on the news! It was definitely him, same voice, and same distinctive face. "That's who it was," I thought, "I knew I'd seen him before!"

Hah, they probably thought that a B&B would be safer than a hotel for a liaison. They just didn't realise that B&B owners are always interested in their guests! I bet, however, that she will never chance that again! To protect their privacy (whether they deserve it or not!), I have never told anyone who it was.

The Monkees

The other famous face I have hosted was a member of the American pop group The Monkees who were at their peak between 1966 and 1971. They also had a very successful comedy sit com series again called 'The Monkees' in the 1960s.

He told me that after splitting up in the 70s, the group did a series of reunion tours with different line ups with varying degrees of success. They were around at the time of The Beatles but although they were one of the biggest selling groups of all time when they broke up, they never again achieved the same following and they made nothing like the money of the Beatles as they did not have professional agents, a fact which they later regretted.

This guy, like many members of pop groups, had succumbed to drink and drugs but did manage to pull himself out of it after a few years of demented suffering. This was achieved by turning to religion for help and with the help of a church group he has turned his life around. He now spends his new life going round schools and children's clubs playing his guitar and mentoring children.

I asked him if he would like to play for me and sing the great Monkee songs. He said he would love to and so he set up in the lounge with his microphone and speakers and plugged in his guitar. What a pity there were no other guests in at the time or we could have had a great concert! He sang one of their best-known songs 'I'm a Believer' (very appropriate!), 'Pleasant Valley Sunday' and 'Daydream Believer' along with others of their songs which I was not so familiar with. I also asked for the signature song of the comedy series 'Heh, heh, we're the Monkees' and I just joined in although everyone knows I am not a singer! At the end we had a great chat over coffee with him regaling me with some of the more repeatable stories of life with the band.

Chapter 26

Woman From the 'Evil' Town

This booking was from a woman who was house hunting and wanted three nights to look for a property to buy in the area.

She sounded quite elderly and as she was coming alone and making the journey by train, I said I would pick her up at the station. She told me that she would be arriving at two forty-five p.m. I was there for the train and waited with my boot lid up for her luggage so that she would see me quite easily. I watched as the train pulled in and then out and I scanned the last of the passengers for a lone lady with luggage. No one appeared. I went to the platform to see if she was waiting there but no. Now what do I do? She hadn't given me any phone number to call so I returned home to see whether there was a message. No. About ten minutes later the phone rang and it was someone from the end of my street who asked if I was expecting a lady named 'Robertson'?

"Yes," I said.

"Well, she is here and seems a bit panicky."

"Oh, good I wondered where she was and couldn't phone her. I'll come and get her right now."

I drove into their driveway and there at their door was a little lady with a shopping trolley! (plus, a small dog which I had agreed to take.) The trolley was all the luggage she had, and it was not fastened at the top as there were layers of plastic tubs of food for the dog and the bag would not close as it was so full. I could see that each tub was labelled with 'Friday evening', 'Sat morning' etc and there were so many there would be very little room for any clothes or other items! I lifted the bag into the boot and as I had to put it sideways to fit it in, some of the tubs fell out. I wondered how many times this had happened on her journey over two trains and a dog to control. She, herself, was a bit lame and to make matters worse she was obviously very forgetful. She started to talk the second she saw me and continued non-stop till we arrived at my house. I didn't even get the chance to ask her where she was going when she had walked down the road. She was going to tell me anyway and had apparently arrived on an earlier train and when I wasn't at the house, she had started to walk back down the road which is half a mile long. She didn't say why she did that or where she thought she was going. Getting tired she had stopped at that house where the owner was kind enough to call me.

She didn't want to go out again that evening as she had brought sandwiches, (more plastic tubs!) and would stay in apart from taking the dog out.

I just hoped she wouldn't come into my lounge later and resume the non-stop chatter. Usually, I enjoy talking to visitors, but this was a non-stop rant about her terrible life and the town she wanted to leave. Luckily, she was so tired after her journey that she stayed in her room (as she informed me the next day).

Unfortunately, there were no other guests staying at the time and so I got the full onslaught of her rants.

At breakfast time she started again, and I made several

excuses about not wanting to burn her breakfast or just needed to let the cat out!

I heard what I thought was her calling for me, so I went through and asked, "Were you calling for me?"

"No," she said, "I was calling Buffy just to let him know I am still here."

My thought at that was that Buffy would think she was calling him and so start scratching at the door! He wasn't whining or anything and maybe hopefully couldn't hear her anyway as he was an old dog.

On going back in to see if she was finished, she started ranting again all about what an 'evil' town she lived in and she just had to leave. According to her the town was engulfed in a cult and she couldn't bear it any longer and had made the decision to leave for good as it was damaging her health and mental health.

"What is the name of the cult?" I asked.

"Oh, it hasn't a name, it's just they are non-Christians." Not a lot of details were given as she went on to talk about her dreadful family and childhood then an abusive husband and now, she needed to leave. She had been seriously damaged by her life's experiences, but I wondered why she had taken so long to 'escape'. She told me she was seventy-nine years of age. Her husband had died a couple of years ago and her children lived in England and didn't visit very often. Some of her friends had either died or moved away and the new neighbours were part of the non-Christians who seemed to be taking over the town. The friends she had left were not keen for her to leave but she was determined as she said she couldn't bear to live there anymore. To leave everything at that age and move to where she had no family or friends seemed a strange move, but she was convinced she was doing the right thing and brave enough to tackle it and so good luck to her.

The weather was particularly bad when she was here, and she had forgotten to pack or wear her waterproof trousers and where could she buy some? I took her to the outdoor wear shop where she found some and then went to the estate agents to house hunt. It was still the holiday between Christmas and New Year and so only one was open. She went out for most of two days trailing around with her dog and trolley and I felt really sorry for her. She decided to leave a day early as she found that most rental places did not take dogs. She had thought to rent a place while she looked for a place to buy.

I took her back to the train station, wished her luck, and wondered whether I would ever see her again. I didn't and she obviously didn't find any accommodation anywhere near as I'm sure she would have come back and told me if she had.

Chapter 27

<u>Wow – Be Grateful for Your Life</u>

This is the saddest story I have ever heard.

    A man appeared at my door one night around nine p.m. I saw him pass the back door at the side of my house, so I went to the front door to call him round. I do not let people in the back door as they would have to come through the kitchen then my office which are both private areas. He was just coming round to the front door, and he asked if I had a room for one or two nights. He had been sent from the Mexican restaurant and I actually thought he was Jose see later, so I said, "Oh I didn't recognise you without your fancy shoes on." I had never seen Jose without them.

    "No," he said. "I'm John, the two guys in the restaurant recommended you and said you were reasonable." Reasonable? Good value or good to haggle with?

    "Ah, OK, I can give you two nights."

    We then agreed a price and he proceeded to tell me his story while still on the doorstep. The way he was speaking I knew he was really upset, and I did not feel like interrupting him. He had a very genuine air about him, so I let him speak.

    His partner had just died, and his mother had died two weeks ago. He had just had the worst two days of his life. About three weeks ago he and his partner had had a 'domestic'. During their altercation he had pushed her too roughly and she fell over. She was not badly hurt but she had him charged with domestic abuse. He was not on bail but was not allowed to contact her. They had a little three-year-old boy who was now staying with his grandmother and the grandmother had banned him from seeing him. They had also taken over his flat, which he had shared with his partner, and they also would not allow him to access his clothes or possessions. He had been sleeping in his van for the past two weeks. He was not eating and had hardly slept. He said he just had to get some sleep and needed a bed. He had no family nearby and the family of his partner would not talk to him.

The way he was speaking it was obvious that he was telling the truth and was in a bad way and genuinely needed to sleep. I couldn't interrupt him to get him inside until he was ready to stop. It was as if he was getting his situation sorted in his mind.

He went on to tell me that on the night when his partner died, he had gone to the shop in the town here where she was working – they had reconciled and were back together but that night she had not come home. He had left several messages on her phone saying he was worried about her. He went to the shop where he found the door locked but he could see that the light was on in the back room. He knew she was in there but could not get a reply. He wanted to break the door down but fortunately realised that he might possibly be implicated if anything was amiss. He called the police who broke in and found her.

He was a broken man and looked as if he could collapse at any moment. He had not been drinking which was surprising in the circumstances.

This was a Saturday, and the autopsy was scheduled for the Monday. He was going to the priest at the church in the morning for help.

While all this story was being related (on the doorstep!), I could not help thinking was this all a tale? However, the details were all there and he was obviously in a bad way, and I could not put him out. I did, however, tell him I could only give him two nights. I would then help him find somewhere cheaper for him. He paid me up front to prove his worth.

He could not even eat a breakfast in the morning or take a cup of tea. He was so physically and mentally upset. It is terrible what can happen to people either by circumstances or their own mistakes.

When he left, he said he would call me and tell me how it all went. He did call and thanked me for my support and he now has access to his son.

It does sound a story which maybe has a lot more to it but I feel I can judge people as to whether they are genuine or not. I did not feel threatened by him and was just horrified at how his life had turned out. One or two wrong decisions can almost destroy your life.

Some of this story was subsequently in the local weekly newspaper about the manager of the paper shop being found in the back shop having died of a heart attack. There was no mention of the man and so he must not have been implicated in her death otherwise it would have been in the local papers and even the nationals.

Chapter 28

Almost a Lodger

Normally I don't take people in long term because I quite like the turnover of different people, different experiences and different stories.

This man never intended to stay so long.

His name was Miguel from Mexico, and he was booked in with me by his friend Jose who lived in Irvine a town about ten miles from here. The friend did the booking as Miguel had no English whatsoever. He was to stay one week or two while he helped Jose with his business. I don't normally take Mexicans either – not because I don't like Mexicans, I do, I find them fascinating, moustaches (usually) and all, but because their connecting flights usually arrive just before midnight and by the time the travellers arrive here it can be one a.m. or later. Because this guy was staying a bit longer than usual, I agreed to take him and stayed up for his arrival. Luckily the flight was early, and he arrived around midnight. He and his friend came in as Jose had collected Miguel from the airport and also Miguel was not able to drive on the 'wrong' side of the road! I showed them to his room, and he produced the week's rent from his pocket and Jose counted it out for me as Miguel did not have the words. Through Jose, who was wearing very trendy shoes (I love fancy shoes), I learned that Miguel would like breakfast at nine a.m. and would have the Continental not the British fry up. He liked espresso coffee. Well, I don't have an espresso machine so I would have to make very strong coffee! Jose told me that would be fine, and he would collect Miguel in the morning at ten a.m. OK, fine. I shook hands with them both and to Miguel I said several 'Si, Si' to the things Jose was saying. This was all very friendly. I felt sorry for Miguel as here he was in a foreign country with a hostess he could not converse with easily and probably had no idea where he was. I don't know if he had been to Jose's house before either.

In the morning when he came down for breakfast, I started my sign language.

"Buenos dias, Miguel," (about the only Spanish I know along with 'nachos' and 'adios'). I asked him if he had slept well, hands together at the side of my face, and also saying, "Has dormido bien? – did you sleep well?" Very proud of myself as I had looked that up beforehand!

"Si, si," he said, smiling. Oh good.

Inspiration—

"Est-ce que tu parles Francais?" I asked him, without much hope. I could have conversed a little more with him in French with my basic French, albeit my school French, which is not great, and, with my French daughter-in-law having parents with no English I had tried a little with them.

Miguel shook his head unfortunately but at least he knew what I had said.

I made him ridiculously strong coffee, being the nearest to Espresso I could do, and gave him white and brown toast having established the night before that he didn't want cereals or even orange juice. Fruit and cheese and cold hams were there too. I would show him an egg tomorrow to see if he would like a boiled egg too. I did not think I could mime an egg, that would be a step too far!

Miguel was a tall lanky guy, mid-forties, and the funny thing was he was the image of a famous Glaswegian comedian Ricky Fulton who did the 'Francie and Josie' shows both on stage and on TV with Jack Milroy. The only thing missing was the trademark curl sticking out of the top of his head! His facial expressions were so like Ricky that I just couldn't stop smiling and could barely keep in my laughter. Shame I couldn't share that with him. What a hoot, this should be interesting!

Jose did collect him at ten a.m. and I gave Miguel a house key so that he could come and go as he liked.

I don't know what work they were doing as he was back at three p.m. and I had seen the two of them in a cafe at lunch time. He came into my lounge and sat down with his phone. Most people don't come in there as they know it is my own lounge and they don't want to disturb me. If they ask if they can come, I say yes, no problem. I did not like to tell Miguel he couldn't come in and so I didn't mind and let him be.

I wondered what he would do for dinner and around six p.m. with no sign of him going out I asked him if Jose was coming to collect him? I pointed at him and said 'You' then pointed at my wristwatch then made my hands mimic driving and actually made vroom, vroom, noises! I chuckled to myself and he stared at me then went on to his phone for help and said, "Tomorrow." I kept on and did signs of eating and pointed at him again and he shrugged his shoulders (he was to do this a lot during his stay!) and said, "No, no." Well, I wasn't going to feed him every day, so I left him to it.

In the next few days when I asked Miguel if Jose was coming for him today, he would say, "Ten," and then when Jose didn't show up at ten a.m., he would say, "Three" or "Five" and shrug his shoulders again. He sat in the corner of my lounge and smiled and nodded every time I passed by. He watched TV all day and discovered the channel for the programme 'Friends' which he would watch for hours. As it is not in Spanish, I don't know how much he understood but he certainly loved it. When Jose didn't show up at all I gave Miguel some chicken and salad as I felt sorry for him.

Why didn't he go out and walk round the area? Why didn't he go out and see where he could eat and what was nearby? After all he had a phone and could answer if Jose or anyone called him. Why did he wait for Jose all the time? He would text his family and also talk to them at length in very fast Spanish. It sounded like his wife was giving him a hard time over the lack of action! I'm guessing of course!

He managed to convey to me that Jose wasn't answering his phone or his texts. What was going on? To add to his misery the weather in Spain was thirty degrees and the weather here was thirteen degrees!

The next time I was going to town I said, "Hola, Miguel, you," then pointing to myself, "come with me to town in the car?" (doing driving motions again)

"Ten minutes?" I held up my hands with ten fingers showing.

"OK," he said.

I dropped him off downtown and indicated the sea front and the railway station. I had given him a street map too to help find his way around.

Well, blow me he was back in about an hour with a bag of pastries. Why didn't he spend the day looking round the town and beach? It was a reasonable day after all. He went back to the Friends channel.

As time went on Jose only came for Miguel occasionally. What was he doing?

At the end of the week Miguel paid for another four nights then another three etc., etc.

I decided to call Jose myself as I could not ask Miguel for any details. He told me that Miguel was hoping to find a flat in Falkirk (Falkirk? That is nowhere near here!) This was proving difficult as he needed a sponsor and a visa, and this was taking time. You're not kidding! I was really no further on in finding out what was happening. I was still sorry for Miguel but wondered why he was not more proactive. Why were the two of them not working together as was supposed to happen?

I got used to Miguel in my lounge watching copious episodes of Friends and also writing long lists of words in two columns of Spanish and English. While he was writing these, I could hear that he was listening to Flamenco music. Maybe it made him feel more at home. I liked it anyway.

He did not seem to be doing proper English lessons with verbs, grammar or sentences. He would speak to me saying 'Lady' and 'I go to my room'. I kept saying to him to call me by my first name and taught him to say 'I AM going to' wherever. At the breakfast table I taught him knife, fork spoon, cup, saucer (he had difficulty with that one, I had to break it down into saw and sir. He managed to learn one word – holding up a cup and saying 'kip' and smiling.

He showed me pictures of his wife and sons aged about

ten and twelve and said that not one of them speaks English. "They, no English, wife, no English." He was beginning to learn a few words of broken English and was able to tell me that me that he and his wife had 'two shop in Mexico'. They were all coming over in July to live here. He arrived in April! He said he was a 'tortilla maker' (of course!) and that he had sold one of his shops to help Jose 'to make a business with him. You help family and friends'.

So, the job and the apartment in Falkirk didn't work out for him and he was going back to Mexico. Good move, Miguel! But he was coming back the next week! What? How I wished I could talk to him properly to find out what this was all about!

Sure enough, the next week he returned on the late night flight and I left the front door unlocked for him as he knew where his room was and it meant that I didn't need to wait up for him.

Now the story, from Jose, was that he and Miguel were looking for a property in this local area to open a Mexican restaurant. Miguel was looking for an apartment/house a little inland a few miles from here and less expensive.

There are already very many successful and popular restaurants all around here and inland and throughout the area with several cafes too so I would have thought that yet another one would have a hard job to survive. Well hopefully they had done their homework and research! The way things were going that seemed doubtful although a Mexican one would be different and interesting and lots of people do like Mexican food.

Again, I had him indoors watching Friends and waiting, sometimes in vain for Jose. What is he thinking? Every time I asked, "Jose, what time?" He would shrug the shoulders again. I asked if he had a sponsor yet?

"Si, si, Jose." You're kidding!

They went to see some properties and managed to find a small house inland. However, it was in a filthy condition, as it had been empty for a long time, but he was going to take it.

"Will Jose help to clean it?"

"No, no." Surprise, surprise!

He paid the deposit but then it took over two weeks to wait for the paperwork and the keys. Hitch?

Suddenly he announced he was going back to Mexico again. Whaat?

He would be back the next week, Jose would phone me for the date and, when ready, he was going to pick up the keys for Miguel's new place.

Well, Jose did not phone and Miguel didn't come back.

Well, I had to know – how did it end? What happened…?

I knew which agent they were using and so out of curiosity I called in.

I explained who I was and how I knew him and that I was concerned for him. It turned out that Miguel had cancelled the rental and got his deposit back. The agent had no more information.

I'm guessing that he had changed his mind about the partnership, and he couldn't call me to explain his absence. I'm sure that he would have if he had had the English to tell me the end of the story. Good luck, Miguel, I hope things got better for you!

Well actually—

Almost a year later, they, the two of them, turned up. Not here, but while I was away on holiday a new small Mexican restaurant opened up a few miles inland fairly near to where

Miguel had been going to live before. It was not in a particularly good location for a restaurant and would need a lot of advertising to get it known. I had settled back into work and had not heard of this new place when a lone B&B guest arrived for three nights. He had eaten at this new restaurant and got talking to the owners. He happened to mention where he was staying and one of them told him that he had stayed here for two months. Miguel's English must have improved!

Well, well, I take it all back! Maybe it's a good partnership after all! I'll need to pay the restaurant a visit…

Still strange – I lunched at the restaurant with a friend and we enjoyed delicious fajitas with unusual and tasty guacamole. Miguel greeted me with, "Hola, Hola, Margaret!" No, his family was not over with him nor coming over. He was now living not far from the restaurant. The location of the restaurant was quite rural, and many people didn't even know it was there (as I didn't). It actually looked very appealing as it had a little brightly decorated straw donkey wearing a sombrero outside the front door! We were the only diners in apart from two shady looking characters dressed in black at the back at a table facing the wall…

Hah, many months later the restaurant has changed its name again, still Mexican…

Well not unexpectedly that restaurant folded. Location must have been a big problem. I do not know where or if they are still around.

Chapter 29

Diets and Nice People

Yes, I would definitely say that at least ninety-five per cent of people who have stayed in my B&B are nice people. If you treat people as you would like to be treated yourself then most people will be nice back. If someone does not want to interact with other people then they prefer to stay in hotels where they can be anonymous and keep to themselves. Most B&B people are happy and willing to share life stories with you and are interested in you and your family.

It is, however, unusual to come across people like Kenneth and Peter. They were booked in by a friend of mine who, along with her sister, had stayed in my self-catering apartment by the beach front every year for nearly twenty years. Margaret lived in Cape Town South Africa and her sister Patricia, lived in Washington DC North America. Patricia now lives in Prestwick here and the friendship continues. They were both born in Scotland and used to meet up in my apartment for a yearly get together and visit old haunts. As sisters they are very different with strong personalities. Patricia is very forthright and says everything 'as it is' (which I like as you know exactly where you are with her). Some people take offence at her abrasiveness, but she does have many friends, so she does just fine. Margaret is much quieter but has a strong will and gives Patricia a good put down now and again. She is also caring and quite funny and I love being in the company of both of them.

Over the years we have become good friends and I even visited Margaret in South Africa in Cape Town when Lorna was seeing a boyfriend who lived there and they had met while both working in New Zealand. I had been invited to visit his parents as things were possibly getting serious between them. I didn't need to be asked twice and happily booked a flight to Cape Town and found an apartment to rent via the internet. It shared the pool with the owner's house and the young couple shared all this with me and it was a perfect place for our stay. Cape Town is a beautiful city and we enjoyed going up Table Mountain in the cable car, seeing 'the Table Cover' which is a straight line of white cloud which often sits on the flat top of the mountain some days and looks exactly like a table cover as it overhangs the top. The large hill in the middle of the city is called Lion Head and the shape of it looks just like the head of a lion. We also had a tour out to Robben Island where Nelson Mandela was incarcerated. That was quite a moving experience as the guide had been in it at the same time as Mandela. This guide did very well out of his tours as at the end of the tours most of the visitors plied him with very generous tips as I'm sure most of us were trying to make up a little for his experiences.

We went to see the penguins come in one night. We had no idea that penguins did this. Normally we would think of penguins living in the snows of Antarctica. I had seen a film of penguins incubating their eggs then sheltering their chicks on their feet on the ice. David Attenborough made a wonderful film about penguins.

About eighty of them arrive every night just south of Cape Town around nine p.m. and hop up over the rocks then across the grass to cross the small road to get under the wire fence and up the hill into the holes where they had built their nests. This is a research station now where there is a visitor centre with screens on the wall showing several nests where you can watch live what is happening underground. Outside a large stand of seats has been erected for about one hundred people to watch this nightly journey. We climbed up and waited expectantly looking out at the dark fairly calm sea. It wasn't long before we saw the little black heads popping up and moving quickly towards the rocks. Soon it looked like there were hundreds of penguins leaping up the rocks and pouring across in front of us. We were sitting at the edge of the stand and could see one which we named 'Wee Jimmy' who did not follow the others across the road but waddled along past the stand and kept on going through the car park then across the road to the field further down. Apparently, he did this every night. The researchers could not interfere but were concerned that he would someday be run over by the cars as he was so small and be unseen by a driver. The young penguins would hear the parents returning with food and made calling sounds in excitement. The parent penguins are not bird brained and knew exactly where their own nests were in the large area where they all live.

It's such a shame that this lovely city is still embroiled in political difficulties. It is disturbing to still see the shanty townships of great poverty not far from the large white people's houses surrounded by barbed wired walls and fences and electric gates.

Patricia moved back to Scotland and now lives only

three or four miles from me. We 'do lunch' quite often. The two sisters, alternate visits to Cape Town and Scotland for Christmas and birthdays etc and visit with me also.

Margaret is a little frail now and her son Kenneth, who also lives in Cape Town, decided to accompany her on the long journey to Scotland as he could work remotely on his laptop. His brother Peter came up from London to join them.

As Patricia has not enough room for them both to stay with her, she booked them in with me (with a large discount of course!) while Margaret stayed with her. Patricia insisted point blank on me being paid something as 'it's business, Margaret!'

The first night, the brothers came into my lounge where I was sitting watching TV and parked themselves down for the evening without a 'Can we join you?' or 'Do you mind if we sit here?'

If they had asked, I would have said, of course, come in, but now I was thinking if this happens every night this could be a problem as they are here for two weeks! What if I don't like them? I would be doing a lot of ironing in the kitchen!

Next, they asked if I would like a wee dram.

I declined with thanks as I am not a fan of whisky.

"Could we have two glasses and some ice please?"

Sounding like Americans...

"Oh, certainly," and off I went to the kitchen.

I returned with said glasses and ice and pulled out a little coffee table and coasters for them. We had a good chat and although that was the end of my TV viewing for the evening, I really enjoyed their company and thought their stay was going to be fine.

Before they retired for the night, I asked them what they

would like for breakfast. They would consult the menu. They wrote it down and handed it to me. I did not look at it as they had said they would likely have the bacon and eggs.

In the morning I was clearing the glasses when I saw a nasty thick white mark on the little polished table despite having put down the coasters. It would not wipe off. Oh no! I didn't say anything and went through to the kitchen.

I checked their breakfast order and they had ordered the bacon and eggs sure enough along with tomatoes and mushrooms. The eggs listed were x 3 for each of them. I have never been asked for three fried eggs from anybody so I wondered if they meant scrambled eggs as that would have been more normal, although still a large portion especially with other items.

When they came in, I asked them if they wanted scrambled rather than fried eggs.

"No," said Peter, "at home I have 3–5 eggs every day." My eyebrows went very high, "Really," I said, "wow, I have never been asked for that before!"

That started a long conversation about their health issues and how they had corrected them with the Ketogenic diet.

Peter was born with Cystic Fibrosis and had had a lung transplant a few years ago. He had splints on his legs (which he showed me) and slept with a mask attached to a machine for his sleep apnoea.

Kenneth had been morbidly obese and had had a slight heart attack. This had scared him, and a friend had recommended the Keto diet which he researched and studied. Peter knew about it and decided that he would try it also. He was not overweight but with his health problems he reckoned that it would help with that too. Within months Kenneth lost all the excess weight and is now a trim very energetic guy of fifty-nine years. Even the loose skin from the lost weight had reduced to negligible proportions. (Not that he showed me!) Quite amazing.

Peter feels so much better with the new regime and they both stick to it very happily with no cravings at all.

After breakfast they moved to the lounge with their laptops as they were working remotely while here. They saw the white mark on the table.

"What's that? Did we do that?" asked Peter.

"I found it last night when I lifted the glasses," I said. Maybe some water or whisky got spilled.

"Oh, we'll have to fix that," said Peter. "We'll get some oil – is there a hardware store near here?"

"Yes, just downtown, thank you so much I'll give you money for the oil."

"No, no, we did that, we'll get oil, sandpaper and dusters and get that sorted for you."

And they did just that.

The coffee table is part of a nest of three tables. There is one long one and two small ones which fit underneath it. Peter and Kenneth ended up spending several hours over the two weeks sanding and oiling all three tables! They decided that having done the one they would do the others to make them all shiny together! Next, they did my cereal cabinet as well! They were also going to do my pine window ledges which had cat scratches on them from years back! Sadly, they ran out of time before they could do those. However, they have left me instructions for doing them.

"When can you move in?" I joked.

Having gone through my entire menu of breakfast options – full Scottish, scrambled eggs (seven!), smoked salmon, kippers (one time they had kippers plus seven scrambled eggs plus bacon!), they started modifying their choices. They would bring in additions as they would have a huge breakfast which they said would last them all day. E.g., an omelette from six eggs plus sliced fried chorizo sausage plus a whole block of grated blue cheese!

A large tub of extra thick Greek yogurt plus one tub of blueberries plus one tub of raspberries each, pouring double cream and mixed nuts and seeds.

They bought several packets of streaky bacon. (British people usually only use streaky bacon for covering a turkey or chopping into a stir fry for flavour because of the extra fat. In North America and South Africa streaky bacon is their normal.) Mind you, I now eat streaky bacon too as I love the crispy fat which, according to the Keto diet is natural and good for you! (They ate a whole packet between them plus two pork sausages for Ken and two beef sausages for Peter, plus mushrooms, tomatoes and sometimes baked beans too.)

When in at night they would snack on different cheeses – blue, brie, camembert, cream cheese, smoked cheddar, prawns and double cream and nuts (almonds, walnuts etc.).

The Keto diet is mainly no carbohydrates i.e., no potatoes, bread, cakes, biscuits, peas (that one is surprising, apparently, they are high in carbohydrates) and definitely no sugar of any kind. Wine, especially red wine, and whisky seemed to be an exception! (Nice one.) No strawberries, grapes, peaches, plums etc. as they are full of sugar. Butter and cream and bacon fat is good for you as it is natural fat. NO processed food of any kind. No margarine or tubs of spreads, everything has to be natural and not processed.

The only meals out they had was when they went with Margaret and Patricia for lunch, and I joined them for two dinners together at Patricia's golf club and another at a wonderful fish restaurant.

This diet obviously works for them and is actually becoming well known as a diet that really works.

Peter was a medical rep until recently and he was telling us that all belly fat is caused by insulin resistance. Carbohydrates are converted to sugar which is poisonous to humans and the body can't get rid of it and so it goes into fat usually round your middle.

I have never met such caring people as Kenneth and Peter.

I put a pile of laundry on the stairs to be carried up next time I was going. My knees hate stairs so I avoid unnecessary trips up. Kenneth saw it sitting on the steps later and took it up for me. (Their room is downstairs). Twice he did that as he knew I struggled. When we had a bad storm the plastic cover of my tomato greenhouse blew off and the uprights came apart. I was out there fixing it (quite happily) when Kenneth appeared saying, "Margaret, Margaret, what are you doing? Let me help you!" He had seen me through the window of the lounge.

One evening I was invited to join them all at a very good fish restaurant. We had an excellent meal and as Margaret does not eat very much, she passed on dessert. The choices were superb and as we were enjoying ours Peter got up and walked round the table to her with a spoonful of his cherry and brandy cream and gave it to her. "Oh, that is so good," she said. How thoughtful. He knew that she had forgotten that she had said she didn't want dessert. Both Kenneth and Peter would help her whenever she needed it and would always help her out to the car and completely look after her.

After the meal, as I was driving, I took them to a nice

hotel on the sea front for coffee and they had liqueurs with it.

It was Patricia's birthday when they were here, and they bought their favourite aunt a gift and flowers. They gave me flowers too when they left and said how much they had enjoyed staying here. Kenneth also put a nice review on Trip Advisor for me. They are such lovely people who adore their families – sharing photos of their children and who just like and care for other people.

I thoroughly enjoyed their visit and would have them back any time.

I must do those window ledges. I will, I will…

By the way, I now do the Keto diet too (except when on holiday or visiting friends or a night out or birthdays…!).

I can confirm it does work. I lost seven pounds in three weeks. I am hoping to lose the belly fat which all women have found almost impossible to shift. The trouble is that I do love my Ayrshire 'tatties' and toast! I just cannot give up those potatoes in June/July when they are at their smallest and most delicious. Toast has been a staple for me for most of my life and that, along with the potatoes, is the most difficult to give up. Cheat days are allowed but the trick is not to have too many! I did lose an inch and a half off my waist but have quite a bit to go yet.

Chapter 30

Sock Droppings

Who knew there was such a thing?

I used to wonder why so many people left tiny bits of black fluff dotted all over the carpet, and in the bed! Eventually I came to realise that most men wear black socks! Who'd have thought or even wondered? They pad about the room and the bits of fluff come off the socks on to the carpet. When in bed the bits come off their feet if they haven't had a shower or a bath.

Although it's nice if guests take off their shoes at the front door it's not so good if they're wearing black socks!

These little offenders are not easy to vacuum away and sometimes they have to be picked up by hand.

Bikers – Fluff?

I had always been scared of bikers. They seemed to me to be big hairy tattooed loud guys who acted like bully boys. I had no reason to change my mind after the supposed wrath of one of them. I was driving home one day when, seemingly out of nowhere, a biker's face appeared right on my driver's window! He had his helmet and goggles on so I couldn't see his face and he was waving with his black gloves and yelling at me. I got the fright of my life! I didn't know what or if I had done something to annoy him or if he was just having a laugh. He didn't look like he was asking for directions! I drove on to escape him and saw in my rear mirror that he was following me. I slowed down and he did the same, I sped up and he did too. Why didn't he overtake me? This kept going on for a few miles and eventually I thought I would head for the police station. He was really making me nervous. A few more miles and he was still tailing me. Just as I was nearing the police station he sped off and turned the other way. Thank goodness.

Soon after, I had a booking for a single guy who didn't tell me he was a biker. He arrived in the evening, as most people do, and as I was in the kitchen preparing dinner, I didn't hear him coming. I went to the door and opening it I saw this guy all dressed in black with helmet and visor still on. Honestly, he looked like Darth Vader! He must have seen my face as he quickly took off his helmet and apologised and said he didn't mean to give me a fright. He had! He was really nice, and I don't even think he had any tattoos at all! He asked if he could put his bike in the garage and I said that would be absolutely fine.

While taking another booking the guy did say they had bikes and asked if I would have space in my garage for four bikes? Thinking they meant bicycles I said no problem.

I heard them before I saw them! Oh no, they were scary men in black! The whole street must have heard them coming! Vroom, vroom, vroom! They came to the front door and asked very politely if I could open the garage for them. I opened up and they just about managed to get the four huge Harleys all in. I admired the shiny black machines and couldn't believe how big and wide they were. I don't think I could have stretched across them! I didn't say this in case they offered to lift me on to one!

They lifted off their panniers, I locked the garage, and we came into the house.

Yes, they were hairy – long hair and thick beards, yes, they all had tattoos, black outfits, black bikes, black gloves and black boots. Really, they all came in looking like Santa Claus in a black suit! However, they were so nice and friendly, quiet and respectful. Just big pussy cats! I would have them back any time and now I am not nervous of the 'Men in Black'.

Of course, they left me some black fluff on the carpet! All is forgiven.

Apart from black fluff another thing I wish people would not do is this – although not using a napkin during their meal, when they are finished eating, they lift a clean napkin out of the pretty box on the table and just dab their mouth with it and put it on their plate. Strangely, I don't mind them using the napkin for the meal, after all that is what they are there for, but I do mind just a dab mark only on the still folded clean napkin! Seems a waste of a napkin but I don't suppose it matters whether it is well used or just dabbed! Just smile and ignore it! It's surprising how many people do this!

Another notable transgression is when people leave the lights on in their room when they go out and also when they leave. It can be the shaver point in the ensuite or the bedside lamps or the main room light or all three! Sometimes people leave the front door open too. Would they do that at home? They can also leave the windows open which can make the house cold as I wonder 'Where is that draught coming from?'

If the light is on too then flies and wasps can come in. One woman broke a cup on the hospitality tray while swatting a wasp in panic – with a shoe!

Another thing you can find is that they have left wet towels on the bed thus making that section of the duvet wet. They just don't realise or think what they are doing.

At breakfast time I put each pot of coffee and tea on a mat to protect the table even although there is a protective cloth under the cover. Probably without thinking they put their pot down on the table cover after refilling their cup.

All these 'crimes' are minor in the scheme of things and I'm just grateful that I have not had (touch wood) any major disasters.

This one most people don't do but I have had a few guests who, when helping themselves to jam, marmalade or honey, will put a spoonful of the preserve on to their plate first before transferring it on to their toast. There is a spoon at each of the preserves so I don't know why they do this other than it may just be a habit. Fair enough, but if using their own spoons, which some people do, then why not put it straight on their toast? It's not as if they are putting their own spoon back into the jam.

It's amazing to see how many guests (usually older people) bring their medication tablets to the table and ask for a glass of water to take them with. I bring one for them and tell them that all cold taps in the house are drinking water taps but if the guests are staying more than night, they still bring the pills to the table. Some have said that their pills have to be taken with food. I'm sure that if they take them as soon as they return to the room that would not be a problem. I know that I would not want an audience while taking tablets!

The number of tablets some people take a day is astonishing. "This one is for my heart, this one for cholesterol, this one for diabetes, these ones for the side effects for those ones," etc., etc. No wonder they don't feel well! I feel like saying to them, "How's that working for you then?"

For some people this leads to a long conversation about all their ailments which they share with the rest of the table.

Other quirks I would never have thought of – some people put orange juice on their cereal. Another one is putting jam on their porridge. Well, if you like it why not? Cinnamon toast anyone?

One morning while going through to take in more coffee I noticed strange looking toast on someone's plate. It was not the colour of any of the jams. I later discovered it was ketchup! That was a first! One thing I have never seen is, even although this is Scotland and I have had many Scottish guests, is anyone putting salt on their porridge! I know my dad put salt on his and it was known then as the thing to do!

It's interesting though to observe people's idiosyncrasies.

Some people just cannot manage my driveway. They would drive in up to the house no trouble at all, but could they drive out again? They would reverse then have to come up again as they were heading for the flower bed. This would be repeated again and again. They used to often drive over the flower bed without realising and leave a trail of broken plants. A friend of mine suggested I put stones along the edge and this I duly did. I collected the largest stones I could carry and painted them white and placed them strategically along the path.

Result!

It is, however, quite entertaining watching the guests heading for the stones and then – thump! The driveway looks straight but there is actually quite a curve on it which you don't notice when you drive in. When reversing you have to turn the wheel to follow the curve back to the road. When driving in you do it automatically while looking at the place you have come to. I have offered to take guest's cars out on the road for them quite a few times. One man came here for many years to play golf and just could not get the hang of the driveway. His pride would not let me do it for him nor would he take my instructions. The secret is to line up the gap in the hedge in the wing mirrors and keep it even on both sides as you go down. No problem. Every year he went up and down repeatedly. He seriously wanted me to cut a couple of feet off the hedge at either side at the bottom of the driveway! I said that that would leave a gap in the driveway and that would have to be filled in with matching mono block. Since the hedge is past the flower bed, I don't think that would make a difference anyway!

One woman gave up on repeated reversing and decided to do a three point turn up at the house. She ended up stuck sitting sideways across the driveway! I had to go out and rescue her and try not to laugh. It would have made a wonderful video on YouTube and would have gone viral!

Chapter 31

Familiarisation Visits

Being a member of the local tourist association has many benefits for all bed and breakfast owners especially for first timers. Not only do they meet fellow owners at meetings, but they can learn many official and personal 'how to do things' and how to deal with different and sometimes difficult situations. Members, if they are full for a night can check the association's website to see who has availability and then direct the guests over there. They would also add their own availability to the website to have people sent to their own place. In the old days it was a case of if full then you phoned round the other B&Bs to find a vacancy. When Visit Scotland had open offices in most towns B&Bs and hotels would phone in their vacancies for the night and tourists would find the vacancies from there. Now Visit Scotland has closed all but the largest town visitor centres with the view that everyone books via the internet. They won't be persuaded that that is all very nice and lovely, but people still want to go into a town's visitors' centre and pick up leaflets for attractions, where to eat, have accommodation found for them, local activities and what's on today! The assistants can tell them particular things about the area and the best way to get to them and find what they are looking for. If you go abroad most places have wonderful and usually large visitor centres.

To my mind if there is no Visitor Centre in a town, then the assumption for a visitor is that there must be nothing of note to see or do, so they will go somewhere else!

Because of this many B&B owners form a local association of their own. Our local association arranges day visits for its members to experience local attractions for themselves so that they can advise and inform their guests on what to see and do. They have also contacted the attractions and persuaded them to give discount tickets for us to give to our guests who are delighted to receive them.

The familiarisation visits are in the off season when we are not so busy. This allows us to meet up with each other and share experiences making them enjoyable social events too.

A trip to Turnberry Hotel, Turnberry being famous for its golf course, was a memorable day experiencing what the hotel resort has to offer. It sits high on the grassy bank with magnificent views over to the Isles of Ailsa Craig and Arran. We competed against each other at air rifle shooting at two different distances and at this I was the winner as my father had two air guns and my sister and I used to set up targets in our back garden for fun. We used empty tin cans on a wall and also old vinyl records and loved when we hit, and they exploded to pieces (little did we know that these same records would have become quite valuable one day!).

We also competed at archery, but I was not so good at this as I had never done it before but still made a pretty good effort. Bows and arrows are heavier than they look!

Quad bikes are available round the grounds too, but we

did not have enough time to do that. We were shown into the spa and pool but again time was not long enough. We were treated to an excellent lunch then shown into the kitchens where it is possible to book for dinner at the Chef's Table which is at one end of the kitchens. From there you can watch the chefs at work and throughout the dinner the head chef comes over to the diners and tells them where the ingredients come from and how the dishes are cooked and created. The day ended with a magnificent afternoon tea sitting at the large windows overlooking the golf course, the sea, and the famous light house. Turnberry golf course is famous for being another course on the list for the Open and being a links course, it has wonderful sea views. The hotel has now become Trump Turnberry and the name Trump is the largest thing you see as you approach the hotel!

Culzean Castle

Not far from Turnberry is Culzean Castle which is the most visited attraction in Ayrshire and owned by the National Trust for Scotland. It sits perched on the cliffs with wonderful views out to Ailsa Craig and the Mull of Kintyre and sunsets over the Isle of Arran. President Eisenhower stayed at the castle during World War II. Nowadays you can rent his apartment for £3000 and up for a week. Guided tours of the Castle take you round the magnificent rooms and original kitchens. With the spectacular setting and photo opportunities it is unsurprisingly a wonderful wedding venue which is booked up years in advance. There is a visitor centre in the grounds with a video presentation and the ubiquitous gift shop. The grounds and gardens are extensive – two hundred and ninety-seven acres, with an extensive play area for children, a swan pond, walled garden and a deer park. There are many walking trails including an access climb down from the cliffs to a little beach where there is a series of caves to explore, an old bathing hut from the 1800s and the formation of a plunge pool which at one time was fed by hot water down from the castle.

Ailsa Craig

Ailsa Craig is a Christmas pudding shaped island just off the Ayrshire coast south of the Isle of Arran. It is an old volcanic plug and is the original place where the beautiful granite was quarried to make curling stones. It is an uninhabited island and a bird sanctuary. The west side of the island is covered in breeding birds with their nests clinging to every crevice on the cliffs. Gannets make up the largest numbers but there are also Herring Gulls, Kittiwakes and if you are lucky, you will spy a few Puffins too. Boat trips can be taken round the island from Girvan with commentary supplied in several languages. Landing on the island is prohibited.

The Isle of Arran

The much larger island of Arran is a magnet for visitors as it is easily accessible by car ferry on both sides of the island. It has been dubbed 'Scotland in Miniature' and is just twenty miles long and ten miles wide with bounteous things to do to keep all ages entertained. The highest point is the mountain Goatfell at 2866 ft and it is one of the four Corbetts (mountains between 2,500 and 3000 feet high) on the island.

Below Goatfell is Brodick Castle originally built in 1510 AD and is now another castle owned by the National Trust. It houses many valuable artefacts and furniture, has extensive gardens where many tropical plants are grown in the sheltered grounds surrounded by woodland trees. By the gift shop there is a plant area selling some of the much sought-after species.

There is a whisky distillery on the north of the island offering tours (and tasting!). There is also a delightful restaurant and of course a gift shop.

You can also visit a cosmetic factory and watch the items being made and of course purchase and then there is the cheese factory making really delicious Arran cheeses. Arran Mustard Cheese is one of my favourites.

At the car ferry terminal at Brodick there is a large visitor centre (the only visitor centre in the whole of Ayrshire!) and a hop on hop off bus going round the island passing through scenic glens with glimpses of deer, pheasants, eagles and many sheep on the hillsides. On the other side of the island there are walks to standing stones and Bruce's cave where Robert the Bruce is said to have come across the legendary spider. Here, at the 'back door' of the island, is the port of Lochranza where another ferry goes to Claonaig, on the Kintyre peninsula on the mainland. Many people stop at this ferry port to see the basking sharks which can be seen swimming around the pier quite often.

On the east coast of Arran opposite Ayrshire is the small island of Holy Isle which is charmingly accessed by a tiny boat with an outboard motor. Situated on Holy Isle right at the ferry landing is a retreat hosted by Buddhist monks at The Centre for World Peace and Health. It can be visited for an afternoon or a holiday break. The time when I and a couple of friends went across to the small island, we were accompanied on the boat by two monks who were dressed in their brown habits and open sandals, and they were carrying and swinging their incense holders. Monks can also be seen tending the large gardens where they grow a large number of vegetables and fruit for their kitchen.

There is another retreat for women only and is at the far end of the island. Just up to twelve women can go there at any one time and they live in the barest of conditions to 'find themselves'. The women stay in the retreat for three years, three months and three days and do not sleep lying down apparently but stay upright. Only essential conversation is allowed and although they are allowed out for gardening, they spend most of their days in prayer.

The rough footpath which is round the edge of the hill to get to the retreat, we found was too far to investigate and get back to the ferry in time. We reckoned we had found ourselves enough for the day!

Back to Arran there are seven golf courses, three of which are eighteen holes, three nine holes and a unique twelve hole and also a crazy golf area. The coast of Ayrshire is very indented and as you travel north or south these two islands seem to change location all the time. It is quite fascinating.

Our group has also been to visit Kelburn Castle near Largs, Dundonald Castle near Troon, Rowallan Castle and golf course near Kilmarnock, the Maritime Museum at Irvine, Burns Cottage and the Burns Museum in Ayr. Another jewel in the crown of Ayrshire is Dumfries House which Prince Charles saved for the nation and now hosts youngsters from home and abroad teaching them agriculture, science technology, landscape design and learning from nature. The magnificent eighteenth-century house sits in two thousand acres of gardens and woodland. Guided tours are available to view this amazing restoration and its unrivalled Chippendale furniture. Dumfries House is also a very popular wedding venue.

Another mansion and grounds well worth visiting is the Neo-Gothic Mount Stuart built for the 3rd Marquess of Bute on the Isle of Bute. This too has large beautiful grounds and the house is famous for its Marble Hall and Chapel with wonderful pink marble columns. The main hall in the house has wall size tapestries and the wonderful massive broad staircase leads up to an upper level with a map of the stars on the neck craning ceiling.

Chapter 32

Princess Scota

There are not many people with whom you feel such an instant connection, but a guest came in with such an amazing story of her life and works that I just wanted to hear more. Her experiences and coincidences in life resonated with me and as none of us had anywhere we needed to be that morning we kept talking.

Personally, I have long felt that a power greater than me has directed my life in what is far greater than mere coincidence. Just one recent example of this is when I was stressing about whether to buy an apartment or not. I have lived in the family home for over thirty years and know that the time is approaching when I will have to downsize. My main hobby is gardening, and I know that I would miss the garden very much and living in an apartment has not the same amount of gardening to be done even with a balcony full of tubs. Having lived in the house for so long all the family memories are here. Not the least of these is the fact that there is a Monkey Puzzle tree which we planted in memory of our son.

I had wondered over the years where I would go after I retired as I would love an apartment with a balcony by the sea but there were none in this town and I wanted to stay locally as I have many friends here. Anyway, back to the coincidence...

One day I was driving home along the sea front and noticed that there was a new sign advertising an apartment building to be built on the site of an old hotel which had been demolished. This new build had balconies! I hadn't been along there for a while but the foundations were in, and the building was already established. Oh my, when did that happen? Balconies! Is this it? Am I ready for this? Can I do it? Should I do it? Am I too late, are they all sold? Oh well I can just go to the agents and have a look at the plans. I probably couldn't afford one, anyway! I went in, received the brochure, prices, and list of apartments still available. There were not many remaining! How long had that sign been up? How did I miss this? Why hadn't I heard about it?

The prices were not as high as I expected and so I had a big decision to make. I struggled with this for a day or two and seeing that the apartments were being snapped up I knew I had to move quickly if I was to get one but was this for me? Now I'm not particularly religious, but I talk to God and his 'angels' regularly to thank them for the good things in my life and to also ask for advice. So, I left it in the hands of the angels! Driving to the agent's office the next day I pleaded with them, "Angels, please give me a sign. I need to know what to do. Please, angels, give me a sign!"

As this was such a huge decision for me, I nervously headed to the estate agents. It is usually almost impossible to find a parking space on the main street where the agent's office is located. Again 'angels, give me a sign please'. As I reached the main street in town where the estate agent's office is my mouth opened in amazement. Although the street parking was nose to tail all the way along there was ONE space. Where? Right outside the agent's office! Wow! I parked, went in, and paid the deposit for the apartment. Wow! I have had many of these 'coincidences' throughout my life, too many to be mere coincidences.

Now this guest had the same kind of experiences in her life and on her first morning after breakfast we, along with the friend who had come with her, had a conversation which lasted till lunch time! This almost never happens because guests arrive for whatever reason and usually go out shortly after breakfast to do what they came here to do. I am usually too busy to spend a lot of time with guests during the day. In this case the ladies were here to go to a concert in the town and that was not till the evening and so she, and her friend, were happy to tell her story after breakfast. I had no one else coming in that night and so I could stay on with them and made some more coffee. As she spoke, I thought that if her experiences had happened to me, I would have found it quite overwhelming. She did too but said she must go along with it because things are meant to be, and everything happens for a reason. Now some people might say a coincidence is just a coincidence but maybe they are not giving it enough attention!

This woman's name is Jane Crawford and she is well known in the town of Lanark in Scotland as 'Scottish Wonder Woman'. She has founded a children's charity, for children from alcoholic homes, drug abusing families and children living in poverty in Scotland.

The town of Lanark has a strong connection with William Wallace the famous Scottish patriot. There is a carving of him in a large niche above the front door of St

Nicholas Church in the town. Edward I, King of England, defeated John Balliol, King of Scotland, in 1296. Following this William Wallace assassinated the English Governor and Sheriff of Lanark in Lanark Castle in 1297 then led his army to victory in the famous Battle of Stirling Bridge.

Wallace's mother was a Crawford and Jane's grandfather was named William Crawford which was the name of the knight, Sir William Crawford, who allegedly commanded the four hundred cavalry to run the English forces out of Scotland after that battle.

Jane hates fighting and violence, but she admires the courage and passion of William Wallace in overcoming adversity. This inspired her to create a charity called 'Wallace's Weans' (Weans being a Scottish name for children) to help disadvantaged children to overcome their problems.

She takes part in large walks and events to raise money and she wears her Wonder Woman costume with added Scottish flags, the Lion Rampart and the Saltire. After the attack on the Twin Towers in New York, she organised a peace walk from London to Lanark with friends and business people from the Wallace Society. Together they had the idea of wearing hats 'Wear a hat for Peace'. An even larger march was organised in New York with the hats, 'Man-Hat-On'. For this march she added the American flag to her outfit. This March can be seen by Googling 'Scottish Wonder Woman in New York.' This March was held on the anniversary of the 11 September atrocities, and this is also the date of the Battle of Stirling Bridge!

Jane wanted to get to New York to tell her story about putting Wallace's fighting to rest with the 11 September connection.

Jane's research and fascination with Wallace led to other instances of discoveries with a link to Scota, an Egyptian princess which, legend has it, led to the naming of Scotland. Scota was the sister of the Egyptian pharaoh Tutankhamun and daughter of Queen Nefertiti. She had to flee Egypt with her family, some say because of the invasion of the Ethiopians. They landed first in Spain then went on to Ireland where Egyptian jewellery has been found, and then they. came to Scotland. They also allegedly brought over the famous 'Stone of Destiny' as written on the Declaration of Arbroath. On a window in Dunfermline Abbey, just north of the Firth of Forth, is a stained-glass window depicting William Wallace. Under Wallace's sword is a maiden he is protecting – Scota.

The Firth of Forth just to the north of Edinburgh has several islands with legendary links to Scota. One of the islands is Lamb Island and it is reputedly said to have Scota's buried treasure there. Uri Geller, the Israeli-British magician, television personality and self-proclaimed psychic has purchased Lamb Island and if there is treasure there, he is determined to find it. With his famous fork bending skills he hopes to dowse (this can find metals and minerals as well as water) and find the treasure. He would then donate it to a Scottish museum. Lamb, Fidra and Craigleith islands have been discovered to be aligned in the same way as the pyramids in Cairo.

Scota was from the Armana Dynasty of Egypt. Armana, amazingly, is Jane's mother's name – a very unusual name for a Scottish lady. Jane's father's name is Dan. Scota was linked to the Tribe of Dan in Egypt. She lived in the Karnak Temple. Jane visited this temple long before she had ever heard of Scota and had the strongest feeling she had been there before. With her long straight black hair Jane looks very much Egyptian...

The Scota story was written by the Abbot of Inchcolm in the large abbey on Inchcolm Island, another island, in the Firth of Forth. Because of its Abbey, Inchcolm is known as the 'Iona of the East.' Colm Cille was the name of St Columba, the Irish monk who settled on the island of Iona on the west coast of Scotland. St Columba built an abbey on Iona where he established a monastic community and converted most of pagan Scotland and northern England to Christianity.

With all her information and many photographs of William Wallace, Scota and also herself, Jane believes it all would make a great movie. She is planning to meet with Mel Gibson who is now a film producer and famous for starring in the movie 'Braveheart', the story of William Wallace. She is determined to meet with him and show him all her photographs and research which by now has become quite a hefty tome. It is years of research and evidence, photographs and stories. Many more than I can write here.

Having decided to do this she wondered how she would get to New York to meet him. She knew that he hosts 'An evening with Mel Gibson' once year but it is very expensive to attend plus funding an air fare.

Yet another coincidence with amazing timing happened when she was gardening at home one afternoon with the radio on. It was a quiz programme on air, and she heard that the prize was a flight to New York with £500 spending money and a Broadway show. Listeners were invited to call in and given a phone number to call. She pulled off her gardening gloves and called with shaking hands and gave her name and phone number. Within minutes they called back and told her that her name had been drawn out of the hat. (Man Hat On)? Next, she was told that she would hear a tune played backwards (!) and if she could identify the band playing, she would get one more question. She listened to the tune and had no idea what it was. Out of NOWHERE the words 'Black Eyed Peas' came into her head. She shouted that into the phone. Question two – what is the name of the song? Again, it happened, it came out of her mouth without her thinking about it – 'I got a feeling' she breathed with a pounding heart. Yes, you guessed it, she was correct.

She raised some extra money and booked up to meet Mel with all her photos and the Scota story. She is sure he will love it having made the films of William Wallace, Robert the Bruce and now – Scota?

Mel Gibson's middle name is Colm Cille…!

I can't wait to hear how it all goes.

After a postponement because of new commitments Mel has had to reschedule the meeting for December and this time it is in Glasgow.

Now, after a year and a half because of the COVID-19 pandemic the event has been cancelled again but she is still collating even more information through her research, and I hope she gets to meet him. Mel has rescheduled the meeting for February and this time it is in Glasgow.

Wonder if I could tag along as an assistant and researcher? Again a postponement – now May.

Chapter 33

<u>Four in a Bed</u>

Have you ever watched the channel four programme 'Four in a Bed' on TV?

It is a favourite programme of mine and it has actually helped me to be a better B&Ber!

Four sets of B&B owners stay in each other's B&B overnight and grade each other on a scale of 1–10 on 'hosting skills, facilities, breakfasts, cleanliness, sleep' etc then pay anonymously in an envelope how much they thought the experience was worth. At the end of the week each owner reads the grades that they have been given and what the visitors didn't like and how to improve. They then open up the envelopes and see how much they have been paid. This leads to many acrimonious conversations as most of them disagree with the criticisms.

After the host has shown each B&Ber into the room the visiting contestants start examining their room. They run their fingers along the tops of pictures and mirrors and bed heads, check under the beds, window ledges and the tops of wardrobes looking for dust. They turn over the duvets and pillows looking for any stray hairs and bathrooms are inspected and the hospitality trays are examined.

This made me check my picture tops and light fittings, in

fact everything in the room, and ensuite. The shower hair traps are cleaned and checked before every guest arrives.

I was surprised at how much more the B&Bers in the programme charge compared with around here. Most of them are in England and also a number of them are actually hotels. The hotels have professional chefs which is really not fair on the normal B&B (mind you, their breakfasts were not usually better than the B&Bs except where they offered a bigger choice of options!). The programme was supposed to be for B&Bs only. The hotels have an advantage where they have staff whereas B&Bs do everything themselves.

It is interesting to see that the places which charge exorbitant prices are not usually the winners as value for money is an issue. Glamping is also highly expensive and is not appreciated usually due to communal showers and toilets and a do-it-yourself breakfast albeit with quality local produce.

I was also surprised too that most of the B&Bers offered just 'The Full English' with any combination of. I like to offer not only the "Full Scottish" with every combination too but also kippers with lemon and tomato, scrambled eggs with smoked salmon, porridge and various cereals and fruits. Available is tea, regular and decaffeinated coffee, hot chocolate, and fruit and spiced teas. White and brown toast is standard and there is also a continental choice of hams and cheeses with croissants or hot morning rolls.

Another surprising thing on the programme is that almost all the B&Bers take the breakfast orders at the table in the morning and pre-orders are frowned upon. Because I am the only chef, I ask for orders the night before and I only once had someone decline as she said she didn't know what she would like the next morning. I do not like to keep people waiting and like to have the food ready at the requested time. This works really well, and I have received many compliments.

I have been asked a couple of times by the makers of Four in a Bed (and my friends!) if I would like to be on the programme but – no way! That would be the day when the breakfast might be a disaster (I would hate being filmed!) or Otto would misbehave or whatever!

Chapter 34

<u>NASA</u>

Some people are so interesting that you really want to hear more of their life stories. I spent almost a whole morning with this couple as they were in no hurry to go out and I had no rooms to do that day.

The husband had just retired from his job with NASA in Madison, Alabama. He had worked both in Alabama, Houston, and Cape Canaveral in Florida. He had been responsible for the Saturn 5 rocket which had propelled the first astronauts to the moon in 1969. He had had the final say that day in the Houston control room on when the Lift was 'good to go'. He said that the tension then the subsequent joy in the room was an emotional experience for everyone there. He and his wife (she worked there too) told me many stories of their work and life which they would not let me write down. One, able to be told story, and was one I can remember is that one of those astronauts was spied on one of the tour buses which take visitors around Cape Canaveral. One visitor on the bus nudged his companion and said, "That man up at the front looks like one of the astronauts don't you think?"

His friend thought so too but thought it couldn't be as why would he be on a tour bus?

At the end of the tour the visitor could not contain

himself any longer and when down from the bus he went over to the guy and tapped him on the shoulder and said, "I'm really sorry to bother you but could you please settle an argument for me and my friend? Are you... by any chance?" The man smiled, and said that actually, yes, he was and that he was taking a friend on the tour as he had not been before and that he himself was interested to see if the tour guide was telling the correct and accurate information. He then said that thankfully, yes, he was!

I tell you, you just never know who will come in next as B&B guests!

Chapter 35

Bed and Breakfast Worldwide

Bed and Breakfast establishments are very popular and best associated with Great Britain. They are found in all towns and villages of the UK. They are almost unknown in the US as there is a plethora of motels with usually room only or with an attached café or restaurant. Some B&Bs are found in Europe with the names Pension(e), Zimmer etc.

Some of the best B&Bs I have found were in New Zealand. Lorna was studying business studies at university and she did an exchange, six months at Dunedin (name connection with Edinburgh) University on the South Island. I was lucky enough to be able to accompany her on her journey over there and helped with her settling in process.

We flew into Auckland North Island and hired a car. They drive on the same side of the road over there and the traffic is much, much lighter making driving a pleasure. We stayed with a friend for one night then set off on our travels south. We took three weeks to cover the North and South islands as we wanted to see as much as we could while we were there. We first visited Hot Water Beach on the Coromandel Peninsula and were amazed to see many people lounging about in self-dug steaming 'baths' all over the beach. Many of those people were drinking wine and beer too! How 'cool' was that? We paddled about and the water was indeed hot. There we also saw lots of dolphins surfing inside the large waves coming towards the shore. That was a memorable day of many.

The B&B we stayed in at Lake Taupo was in a beautiful house on the lake side. The lake is so large it looks like the ocean. The owners had a golden Labrador puppy which they were training to be a guide dog for the blind. He wore a special coat to show that he was a dog in training. He was calm and friendly and would make a wonderful companion for his owner to be. The morning after our bounteous breakfast, the owners asked us if we would like to come with them on their boat. They also ran a boat tour company on the lake. They were taking the pup on the boat for the first time to get him used to different situations. We said we would be delighted and really enjoyed the experience. They took us right up close to very large Maori carvings on the rocks and these could be seen for quite some distance away. They were of white and coloured faces, and we could not think how the carvers could have done these as the cliffs are high and vertical.

This is typical of New Zealand B&Bs as they include their visitors in their lives if wanted, and mostly they share their evening meal with visitors too, at no extra cost. Another family had a tennis court in their garden and on discovering that Lorna was a tennis player, the father asked her if she would like a game. She accepted and enjoyed the match even if she just lost, but it was close.

Another B&B had a hot tub in their garden, and this was fed from an underground spring. They filled it for us and then they had to add cold water as the water was too hot to go into! No big electricity bills there then! After leaving this B&B, we went to Rotorua where the famous geysers are. You can actually smell the town before you get there as the smell of sulphur from the geysers is very strong. It is an amazing sight to see the geysers shooting high in the air at random and there is a one-and-a-half-hour trail around the bubbling pools. Along the trail there are warning signs every few yards for people not to go off the trails because if they fell into a pool they would not be seen again! Dogs obviously are not allowed there. Lorna tried the outdoor mud bath, but I just had a paddle in the mud!

We travelled on to Wellington harbour where we had to hand in our hire car and pick one up at the other side – South Island. The ferry does not take cars. It does, however, take sheep! They were on the lower deck and if you looked over the rail at the back you could see the sheep crowded in below. The smell was strong! The first B&B we stayed at was a working sawmill. The owner gave us a tour of the sawmill and it was interesting to see how it all worked and the complicated machinery used. The evening meal was provided here too.

Whale watching is very popular in New Zealand and we wanted to go on a trip as we had never done that before. We signed up for the trip for the next day at Kaikoura on the east coast. The next day dawned but the weather had deteriorated and when we arrived at the jetty, we were told that the trip was cancelled. However, just along from there was a helicopter pad advertising tours for whale watching. We checked that out and found that they were still going. We decided to hang the expense and go for it. We might never have the chance again. It was just the two of us onboard and the pilot who spoke to us through our headphones. It was not a bumpy ride thankfully and we saw four Sperm whales. The pilot knew how long a whale could stay under water and so could point to where and when they would appear. It was fascinating and well worth the trip.

Next, we stopped in Christchurch at another lovely B&B with dinner and were amazed at how British the city was. The street names are taken from Britain e.g., Glasgow St, Manchester St, Cambridge Gardens, Devon Road, Halifax way, Norfolk Avenue and Queen's Road to name just a few. The Avon River runs through the city, and we went punting just like in Cambridge! The wonderful Cathedral in the Square was so beautiful, and it is such a tragedy that an earthquake in 2011 almost destroyed it completely. Due to the danger of subsequent shocks and discussions as to how to fund and do the restoration the work did not properly start until 2017. Up till now in 2021 it is still not complete.

Just south of Christchurch we went to see the Moeraki Boulders on Koekohe beach between Moeraki and Hampden (another British name). These are giant completely round stones on the sand at the water's edge. They are completely natural and have become a tourist attraction. There is a local story saying apparently that many years ago some people attempted to crack open some of them thinking that they may have contained aliens from a far-off planet!

It was the beginning of winter when we arrived at Lorna's lodgings and as there was no heating in the bedrooms we had to go out and buy a fan heater, bedding and a hot water bottle for her! We were amazed to discover that most houses in New Zealand had no central heating! I stayed one night, and in the morning before I left, we had a look round

Dunedin. We saw the University and the public gardens where there is a huge bronze statue of Robert Burns – much larger than any here! The railway station is magnificent. It has a wonderful mosaic floor of 750,000 Minton tiles, pink granite supporting pillars and a frieze of Royal Doulton porcelain running round the balcony.

Too soon it was time for me to leave. I had to drive from Dunedin back to Christchurch to catch my flight to Auckland for the long trip home. I cried all the way to the B&B where we had stayed a couple of nights before. At one stage I had to pull in at an entrance to wipe my eyes. There was a large sign at this entrance saying 'St Andrews Golf Club'. Wow, this country is so like home – not even half the population, better weather, quiet roads and is safe. My baby will be fine. It was really hard to leave her on the other side of the world!

The owner of the B&B welcomed me back and I'm sure she guessed that I had been crying. She told me that dinner would be ready in half an hour, and I enjoyed a great meal chatting to her and her husband and we exchanged many stories of life as a B&Ber.

The B&Bs of New Zealand offer far more than the ones here and give such a good impression of the country and its people. I now offer more little extra touches and a larger breakfast selection and a packed lunch on request. To be a B&Ber is a rewarding occupation especially if you can just 'go with the flow'.

Bed and Breakfast is now changing. 'Airbnb' has evolved into a global phenomenon. It started out with households giving up a room on a room only basis. This was a cheaper option than the traditional B&B. It is now very popular especially with business travellers and young people who are not bothered about a breakfast. There are no regulations governing Airbnb and no inspections are done. This has led to some quality issues. It has evolved again with many places now offering an optional breakfast. This, as you can imagine, has created a great deal of friction within the B&B community and now new regulations are being brought in to cover all Airbnbs too. Many B&Bs have decided that if you can't beat them join them, and so are advertising themselves on the Airbnb website.

With the onset of COVID-19, room only has become the new norm for B&Bs and many places like my own have closed down. When all is opened up again, I'm sure that the room only option will prevail but hopefully Bed and Breakfast will return to normal eventually.